Messages from Quran

A Divine Resilience Model

Dr. Ashi Ezz

Copyright © 2024 by Dr. Ashi Ezz

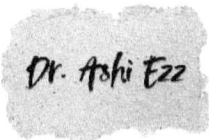

Thank you for purchasing an authorized edition of this book. Copyright fuels creativity, encourages diverse voices, promotes free speech, and contributes to a vibrant culture. By complying with copyright laws and not reproducing, scanning, or distributing any part of this book in any form without permission, you are supporting writers and allowing the continuation of publishing works for every reader.

First edition

Paperback ISBN: 978-1-0670358-6-0

Kindle & EPUB ISBN: 978-1-0670358-5-3

While the author has made every effort to provide accurate Internet addresses at the time of publication, neither the author nor the publisher assumes any responsibility for errors or changes that occur after publication. The author also does not have any control over and does not assume any responsibility for third-party websites or their content.

For inquiries, further information, please contact:

Email: ashiezzpublish@gmail.com

Dedication

In the name of our Lord, the Creator of all, though many walk blind to see the truth's call. It's not the eyes that fail to see, but the hearts that lose its way. This book, Messages from the Qur'an, is a gift to humanity, a lift for the soul in times of calamity.

Like a quiet anchor in a stormy sea, it speaks to resilience in a chaotic world. It reminds us that all things, no matter how scattered, return to Allah; unfurled, revealed, in perfect order. Inspired by Adham Sharqawi's work, it filters through the noise, focusing on the essence that touches the heart and refines the soul.

In my pursuit to build a fortress of resilience, I turned to the Qur'an, seeking its wisdom as the cornerstone. What I found were not just verses, but revelations; a roadmap for those lost in the storm. It's more than ink on a page; it's a guide for the soul, a compass that points us back to our inner strength. The Qur'an doesn't just speak; it transforms. Its message is timeless, calling each of us, no matter the age, to find grace in struggle, power in humility, and peace in surrender. This is resilience, not as a theory, but as a way of being.

In the footsteps of mercy, we find our way, no matter the trials that come our way. For Allah, the Most Merciful, always sends signs to return to Him; the source of all love, where our purpose aligns.

Declaration

I have endeavored to translate these teachings into English to the best of my ability, striving for accuracy in understanding. Yet, remember that the ultimate truth lies within the original texts. Seek refuge in the Quran and the authentic Hadith, for they illuminate the path.

I cannot emphasize more the importance of returning to original sources; the Quran and authentic Hadith in the Arabic language versions; for ultimate clarity and truth.

The Qur'an, as Allah's divine word, cannot be fully captured in any translation; only its meaning can be conveyed. As the Italian saying goes, "Traduttore, traditore"; "The translator is a traitor"; reminding us that some depth and nuance are always lost. We strive to interpret the meaning faithfully, but the true essence remains in the original Arabic

If I am correct, it is from Allah, and if I am wrong, it is from myself and Shaytan. Allah and His Messenger are blameless from my errors.

Contents

Introduction 1
Seeking Knowledge as Resilience (Ilm) 4
Resilience Through Intention (Niyyah) 18
Resilience Through Submission (Tasleem) 20
Resilience Through Everything is Written (Qadr) 26
Reliance on Allah (Tawakkul) 28
Endurance through Testing (Balaa) 34
Resilience Through Patience (Sabr) 38
Resilience Through Perseverance (Mujahada) 45
Forgive One Anther (Afw) 50
Steadfastness (Istiqama) 52
Hope and Optimism (Husn al-Dhann) 56
Resilience through Community (Ummah) 58
Endurance in the Face of Loss 64
Lessons from the Prophets 67
Humility (Tawadu) 79
Self-Restraint (Taqwa) 83
Courage in Adversity (Shuja'a) 86
Resilience in Leadership 89
Resilience Though Overcoming Despair (Ya's) 93
Resilience Through Obedience to Allah (Ita'at Allah) ... 98
Moderation and Balance (Wasatiyyah) 101
Patience in Justice (Adl) 104
Resilience in Family Ties (Silat Ar-Rahm) 106
Patience in the Face of Injustice 109
Resilience Through Contentment (Rida) 113
Patience in Dawah (Calling to Faith) 116
Resilience in Economic Hardship 120

Resilience Through Managing Fear 122
Trials as Purification (Tazkiyah) 126
Resilience Through Perseverance in Worship (Ibadah) 134
Resilience in Speech (Qawlan Sadida) 136
Resilience in Physical Health 141
Resilience Through Remembrance (Dhikr) 143
Resilience in Facing Oppression and Tyranny 146
Resilience Through Charity (Zakat and Sadaqah) 149
Resilience in Building Societal Bonds 152
Resilience in Ethical Conduct (Husn al-Khulq) 157
Resilience Through Gratitude (Shukr) 163
Resilience in Facing Temptations 170
Resilience Through Silence and Thoughtful Reflection 173
Resilience Through Being Dutiful to Parents (Birr al-Walidayn) 177
Resilience in Brotherhood and Sisterhood (Ukhuwah) 179
Resilience Through Repentance (Tawbah) 184
Resilience Through Balancing Worldly Life and the Hereafter 190
Epilogue 197
Final Inner Dialogues 206
The Book Cover 234
Acknowledgments 235
References 236
About the Author 237

Introduction

First and foremost, let me be clear: this book isn't a guide for religious rulings, nor a map for what's halal or haram. It's a reflection, a journey into the patterns of resilience woven through the Quran, viewed through the lens of systems thinking. What you'll find here are insights; not directives; born from my understanding. I'm not here to dictate interpretations or issue decrees, but to share a perspective, one that I hope will spark thought, growth, and a deeper appreciation for the complexity and wisdom that resilience offers us all.

After writing my book on the most influential person on Earth, Muhammad, and together developing the Muhammad's Lasting Resilience Model (MLRM), I felt a pull; almost like gravity; toward the Quran. I wanted to see what it had to say about resilience. And I wasn't disappointed. What I found was a fortress of strength, a castle of resilience, only growing stronger with time.

Introduction to the Divine Resilience Model (DRM)

In a world teeming with challenges and uncertainties, resilience stands as a cornerstone for thriving individuals and communities. Inspired by the timeless wisdom of the Quran and the insightful work "Messages from the Quran" by Adham Sharkawi, this book introduces the DRM. This unique framework, crafted through the lens of systems thinking, meticulously analyzes 45 key themes of resilience found in the Quran, offering a profound understanding of how divine guidance shapes our ability to navigate life's adversities.

The Quran transcends its role as a religious text, serving as a comprehensive guide for personal and communal development. Each verse is a beacon of lessons that encourage self-reflection, instill hope, and foster resilience. In this book, we embark on a journey together, exploring themes such as the power of knowledge (Ilm), the strength of intention (Niyyah), the importance of community (Ummah), and the transformative nature of forgiveness (Afw). Each theme is supported by relevant verses, allowing readers to experience the Quran's teachings in a practical, relatable manner.

As you delve into the pages of this book, you will uncover not only the core principles of resilience but also practical applications that can be seamlessly integrated into daily life. The DRM invites you to rethink adversity, transforming it into an opportunity for growth and spiritual elevation. This framework empowers you to harness the divine wisdom of the Quran, cultivating resilience that uplifts you personally and strengthens your connections with others.

Prepare to embark on a transformative journey where the wisdom of the Quran meets the innovative approach of systems thinking. Together, we will unlock the secrets of resilience, helping you navigate challenges with confidence and grace. Embrace the teachings within, and discover how the DRM can guide you toward a more resilient and fulfilling life.

Without further ado, let us delve into the insights I have uncovered and explore the themes of resilience within the Quran.

Seeking Knowledge as Resilience (Ilm)

Theme: Knowledge equips individuals to face challenges with wisdom, fostering resilience.

Key Verse: *"Say, 'Are those who know equal to those who do not know?'"* (Surah Az-Zumar 39:9)

Echo Verse 1 from surah Al-Alaq

96:1 Recite in the name of your Lord who created

The first word of the Qur'an is "Read," not "Pray." Why? Because acts of worship must be rooted in knowledge and belief.

Prayers without knowledge becomes yoga.

Fasting without knowledge, no more than a diet. Hajj without knowledge, mere steps towards weight loss.

Jihad without knowledge and belief turns into extremism and terrorism.

Trading without knowledge, possibly will end up being forbidden and usury.

Indeed, Allah is not worshipped through ignorance. The noble book that guides us does not permit its companions to remain ignorant or driven by mere desires.

Messages from Quran *Dr. Ashi Ezz*

Echo Verse 2 from surah Al-Baqarah

2:2 This is the Book about which there is no doubt, a guidance for those conscious of Allah –

True knowledge and true religion; these are companions, never in conflict. For while science has revised itself time and again on a single point, this book, the Qur'an, has remained unchanged in my hands for 1400 years. And the more science grows, the more it testifies to the majesty of this timeless truth. Yet, it takes scholars of depth and insight to grasp it fully.

Pity those who limit their belief to what their senses alone reveal; they are poor indeed. They deny Allah because they cannot see Him, yet believe in ultraviolet rays, which they also do not see. They dismiss angels because they cannot behold them but accept infrared rays, invisible to the eye. They forgetting how, when their science once claimed the Earth stood on a bull's horn, our Qur'an declared that all things swim in an orbit.

In an age when their science was mired in superstition and magic, our Qur'an was already speaking of embryos and the stars' precise positions. The religion that made the pursuit of knowledge obligatory could never stand against true science, for that would be a rebellion against itself. But it stands firm against any science that denies Allah's sovereignty over the universe; a foolish science, blind to divine order, that claims the universe birthed itself simply because it lacks the wisdom to offer a better answer.

History proved that the brightest age of science dawned when Muslims held its reins, for then it was wedded to faith. Science without faith is like a body without a soul, and faith without knowledge is like a soul without a body.

Echo Verse 114 from surah Ta-Ha

20:114 and say, "My Lord, increase me in knowledge."

This verse stands apart within the Quran, urging not just fervent prayers or generous charity but beckoning us to delve deeper into understanding the world and ourselves. It reminds us that true resilience springs from the well of knowledge, and what greater wisdom exists than that of our Creator and Lord?

In our pursuit of knowledge, we cultivate an inner strength; a resilience that lifts us above adversity. Each insight deepens our bond with the Divine and enriches our capacity to confront challenges with courage and grace. By nurturing our minds and spirits through the quest for understanding, we honor this sacred call, transforming our insights into sources of strength and inspiration.

Let us celebrate this verse as a guiding beacon, illuminating our path toward growth and enlightenment. In our quest for knowledge, we unearth the tools to build resilience, allowing us to thrive in an ever-changing world, confident in the love and wisdom of our Creator.

Echo Verse 9 from surah Al-Isra

17:9 Indeed, this Qur'an guides to that which is most suitable and gives good tidings to the believers who do righteous deeds that they will have a great reward.

The verse serves as a radiant beacon, illuminating the path that resonate with our well-being and moral integrity.

Through this divine guidance, resilience flourishes, empowering believers to navigate the intricate tapestry of life's complexities with unwavering purpose.

When individuals tread upon a path deemed suitable, they cultivate the strength to endure hardships, reassured that their choices align with righteousness.

Echo Verse 7 from surah As-Sajdah

32:7 Who perfected everything which He created and began the creation of man from clay.

Allah, the Almighty, created Adam, peace be upon him, from clay,
And from Adam's rib, He brought forth Eve.
If Eve is a part of Adam, then Adam encompasses all of her.
Adam, shaped from dust, while Eve, crafted near the heart.

That is why she can find her fulfillment not in power, but in love.
Her true self emerges in nurturing, becoming a compassionate wife.

Motherhood, the pinnacle of love, defines a woman's purpose,
A man weaves a woman into his life; she is a fragment of his being.
In love, a woman makes a man her entirety, her soul's essence.

Filling the void in man's life with her greatest calling.
A woman, proud in her role, aids a man with grace,
For she is of the heart, cherishing his every effort.

A man must soothe her spirit and honor her essence,
Nurturing her femininity to help her truly thrive.

Echo Verse 1 from surah Al-Muzzammil

73:1 O you who wraps himself [in clothing],

When he descended from the cave, trembling with fear, drenched in sweat, he did not seek out his uncle Hamzah, the lion hunter, for protection.

He did not turn to his loyal friend Abu Bakr for comfort. Nor did he go to Dar Al-Nadwah, where the leaders of Quraish gathered, hoping for their solidarity.

Instead, he went to Khadija. She was more than his wife; she was his refuge.

Khadija was his father he had never known, the mother he had lost too soon, and the grandfather who could not raise him. She was the siblings who never came into this world. His loyalty to her was unparalleled, for in her lifetime, he never took another wife.

Some women make others mere numbers, but Khadija was beyond comparison. Even Aisha, in her youth and beauty, felt the weight of her presence from the grave, asking, "Do you still remember her, when Allah has given you better?" To which he replied, "By Allah, He has not given me better than Khadija." Such loyalty; how could a living soul erase the memory of the departed?

Messages from Quran — *Dr. Ashi Ezz*

With ten fingers, she lit his path. And when he was over sixty years old, he saw her companions and honored them, letting the elders sit in his presence. When others marveled at this, he simply said, "These are the companions of Khadija."

Solid acknowledgment from the prophet of women's role in building the foundation of this faith, and refining the resilience of all men.

Echo Verse 36 from surah Al Imran

3:36 But when she delivered her, she said, "My Lord, I have delivered a female." And Allah was most knowing of what she delivered, "And the male is not like the female. And I have named her Mary, and I seek refuge for her in You and [for] her descendants from Satan, the expelled [from the mercy of Allah]."

The "kaf" in this Arabic verse symbolizes likeness, not hierarchy. It's not meant to degrade but to highlight differences. Women excel in some areas, just as men do in others. Claiming men are superior across the board is a biased misinterpretation. Both genders are halves that complete each other, forming the cycle of life. When Allah notes their distinctiveness, it's meant to honor, not diminish, either gender.

Demanding absolute equality that strips away unique qualities diminishes women, reducing them to mere vessels of procreation, neglecting their full dignity and strength. Islam values the equality of all in human worth, but men and women remain distinct, with roles aligned to their nature.

For instance, Islam exempts women from jihad, not out of weakness, but out of honor. Their tenderness and compassion complement their role. Stripping away femininity denies the beauty in their essence.

Yes, the male is not like the female; this is a celebration, not denigration. Women are more tender, enduring, and patient. They bear the pain of childbirth and transform it into love, nurturing life. While men build and fight, women are the pulse of love, providing what the world truly lacks.

Do not let them rob you of your femininity in the name of equality. Stay women, be proud, and defend fiercely your right to be who you are; delicate, strong, and irreplaceable.

Echo Verse 25 from surah Maryam

19:25 And shake toward you the trunk of the palm tree; it will drop upon you ripe, fresh dates.

Allah, in His infinite wisdom, knew full well that no strong man could shake a palm tree, much less a woman fresh from childbirth. Yet, He said to her, "Shake," not out of need, but to remind us of the path of effort; teaching that striving is a vital thread in life's fabric.

Allah provides the worm to the bird, the grain to the sparrow, but never places it directly in their beaks. He, who miraculously gave Mary a child without a husband, could have made the dates fall at her feet without her touch. Yet, the Divine teaches us that our effort is required; not for the result, for the cause itself is but a vessel; empty of power to help or harm.

Let this ignite our quest to understand resilience; and seek wisdom from our Creator's book.

Echo Verse 22 from surah An-Naml

27:22 But the hoopoe stayed not long and said, "I have encompassed [in knowledge] that which you have not encompassed, and I have come to you from Sheba with certain news.

When a hoopoe uncovers what was concealed from a prophet, it imparts a profound lesson: to remain humble about the knowledge we have yet to attain, rather than solely basking in what we think we know.

As the wise Abu Nawas aptly stated, to those who presume they know it all, you may possess some knowledge, yet much remains beyond your grasp.

Echo Verse 23 from surah Maryam

19:23 And the pains of childbirth drove her to the trunk of a palm tree. She said, "Oh, I wish I had died before this and was in oblivion, forgotten."

There are moments when the world tightens before our eyes,

When it feels as though the weight of this vast planet presses upon our chest;

Not for lack of faith, but from the sheer harshness of life's trials.

Mary, steadfast in her belief and trust in Allah,

Faced a burden beyond measure. Her test was profound;

A child born without a father,

And soon, she would stand before a people with hearts hardened by doubt.

In those moments, she tasted the bitterness of the world.

At times, life's blows seem to break us,

And the days grow heavy, stretching on as if they will never end.

This is a part of our humanity; embrace both its powerful and vulnerable moments, confront challenges, and overcome them.

But within your humanity; whether in your frailty or strength;

Hold fast to Allah, acknowledge his divine power. For in every state,

He is with you, as you are with Him.

Resilience Through Intention (Niyyah)

Theme: True resilience is found in doing everything, including facing adversity, with the sincere intention to please Allah. Every act, struggle, and patience become a form of worship when aligned with the right intention.

Key Verse: "And they were not commanded except to worship Allah, being sincere to Him in religion, inclining to truth." (Surah Al-Bayyinah 98:5)

Echo Verse 47 from surah Saba

34:47 Say, "Whatever payment I might have asked of you - it is yours. My payment is only from Allah, and He is, over all things, Witness."

The truest reward comes solely from Allah.

A wise man was once asked, "Is there anything more detestable than miserliness?"

He replied, "Yes, it is when a benefactor speaks of his own generosity."

Remember Allah in every act of goodness, expecting no praise, seeking no applause. Do not look for reward from the hands of people, for every deed done for them is theirs, and every deed done for Allah is His.

It is a frightening thought, as Ibn al-Qayyim wisely said: " if your actions are not purely for the sake of your lord, then save yourself the exhaustion; That's why you may see two people standing shoulder to shoulder in prayer; one earns countless rewards, while the other gains little or none. It all depends on the purity of intention and the presence of the heart.

Let your heart be solely for your Lord, and let your deeds be only for His pleasure, for in this sincerity lies the true worth of your work.

This is the grace of Allah, given to whom He wills, based on sincerity, not mere outward actions.

Resilience Through Submission (Tasleem)

Theme: Complete submission to Allah's will in all affairs provides emotional resilience, as one accepts the divine plan.

Key Verse: *"And who is better in religion than one who submits himself to Allah while being a doer of good..."* (Surah An-Nisa 4:125)

Echo Verse 60 from surah Al-Ankabut

29:60 And how many a creature carries not its [own] provision. Allah provides for it and for you. And He is the Hearing, the Knowing.

Observe the creatures that surround you: birds, fish, frogs, snakes, even the smallest bacteria. None wear garments with pockets, hold bank accounts, carry health insurance, or receive a salary.

Yet, as old age creeps in, they rise each morning, full of confidence in their Lord's provision. Not a single one perishes from hunger.

So, place your trust in Allah. Reflect on the story shared by the wise: Solomon, peace be upon him, once asked an ant, "How many grains do you eat in a year?"

"Two grains," she replied.

So he placed her in a box with two grains. After a year, he found only one grain consumed. He asked her why.

"When my affairs were in Allah's hands, I knew He would never forget me," she explained. "But when my sustenance became dependent on you, I feared you might."

Let this be a lesson: entrust your life to the One who never forgets.

Echo Verse 102 from surah As-Saaffat

37:102 And when he reached with him [the age of] exertion, he said, "O my son, indeed I have seen in a dream that I [must] sacrifice you, so see what you think." He said, "O my father, do as you are commanded. You will find me, if Allah wills, of the steadfast."

One of the greatest trials known to mankind is that of a venerable prophet, deprived of children for years. When finally blessed with a son, his heart filled with love and attachment, the command came to sacrifice him. He did not waver, nor did he delay. He knew well that the visions of prophets are divine revelation, even if they conflict with the deepest desires of the heart.

But Allah, the Most Merciful, would never allow His prophet to slaughter his son. Instead, He was teaching him a profound lesson; to detach his heart from all but Allah, even from the one most beloved to him, and to place his trust fully in the Lord of all.

Echo Verse 86 from surah Yusuf

12:86 He said, "I only complain of my suffering and my grief to Allah, and I know from Allah that which you do not know.

*I confide my grief and sorrow only to Allah;
For to seek pity from people yields mere sympathy,
But to complain to Allah brings forth boundless mercy.*

*The weak do not turn to the weak, for all are frail.
The poor do not seek from the poor, for all are in want.
The powerless find refuge in the Almighty,
And there is no strength greater than Allah.
The destitute seek shelter in the Provider,
And there is no wealth richer than His.*

*Before Allah, show your weakness;
weep, complain, plead, and ask; he is the King of Kings; this rise you even more.
But to the world, raise your head and speak,
remember, everyone else is just like you, creation.
Though your wounds throb beneath the surface.
For every look of pity from people, is another fracture,
And every shoulder leaned upon from creator is another stumble.*

Draw strength from the Divine. Help from others? Sure, but remember; they're just steps.

Echo Verse 5 from surah Fatir

35:5 O mankind, indeed the promise of Allah is truth, so let not the worldly life delude you and be not deceived about Allah by the Deceiver.

Ask Noah of his thousand years on earth,
He'll tell you: life is fleeting, no matter its span.
Ask Solomon, who commanded the winds and jinn,
He'll say: man is ever poor, despite all he owns.

Seek David, whose hands bent iron with ease;
Even strength will whisper, man is weak.
Turn to Pharaoh, swallowed by the sea,
He'll tell you: salt's bitter taste erased his might.

Ask Nimrod, felled by a gnat's hum,
He'll speak of pride; how sandals crushed his crown.
Ask every tyrant, every soul who defied,
They'll tell you the same: do not trust this world's lies.

Echo Verse 31 from surah Al-Muddaththir

74:31 And none knows the soldiers of your Lord except Him. And mention of the Fire is not but a reminder to humanity.

With water, He avenged Noah's plight,

with fire, He revealed Abraham's truth and might.

With lice and blood, He stood with Moses,

His answer can be anything, summoning forces divine; water, fire, locusts, and creatures entwined.

The universe beckons, each a part, Drumming in war with a unified heart. His command echoes clear: "Be," and it is so, A testament to power, a radiant glow.

Resilience Through Everything is Written (Qadr)

Theme: Qadr, which signifies divine predestination, this principle fosters resilience by reassuring individuals that, despite difficulties, there is a higher purpose and wisdom in all occurrences. This perspective allows individuals to remain steadfast, as they understand that their struggles are part of Allah's greater plan.

Key Verse: "Indeed, We have created everything with predestination."

(Surah Al-Qamar 54:49)

Echo Verse 71 from surah An-Nahl

16:71 And Allah has favored some of you over others in provision. But those who were favored would not hand over their provision to those whom their right hands possess so they would be equal to them therein. Then is it the favor of Allah they reject?

Allah does not grant wealth to the sinner out of weakness, nor does He withhold it from the obedient due to any lack; Glory be to Him. This life is but a testing ground. He gives and withholds by His infinite wisdom, not by any measure we understand.

What is destined for you will find its way to you, even if the entire world conspires to block it. And what is not meant for you, you will never attain, even if the whole world rallies behind you. The pens have been lifted, and the ink on the decrees is dry; what is written is certain, and His wisdom prevails over all.

Reliance on Allah (Tawakkul)

Theme: Trusting that Allah's plan is always for the best, no matter the situation.

Key Verse: *"And whoever relies upon Allah - then He is sufficient for him."* (Surah At-Talaq 65:3)

Echo Verse 164 from surah An Nisa

4:164 And [We sent] messengers about whom We have related [their stories] to you before and messengers about whom We have not related to you. And Allah spoke to Moses with [direct] speech.

. *If people are ignorant of your grace, do not despair,*

For it is enough that Allah knows who you are.

Nothing adds to Noah's scale because we know his name,

And nothing is decreased for prophets unknown, their worth the same.

Twenty thousand warriors in Harun al-Rashid's grand array,

Their names unwritten, their salaries forgone, in secret they stay.

Known only to Allah, their deeds in silence shine,

Their valor and faith, a testament divine.

Echo Verse 62 from surah Yunus

10:62 Unquestionably, [for] the allies of Allah there will be no fear concerning them, nor will they grieve

Recall the tale of Joseph, where the caravan's arrival was not by their own design, nor did the man drop his bucket by mere chance.

The Egyptian minister did not purchase him out of desire; instead, all unfolds by divine decree.

For truly, the believers of Allah harbor no fear, nor shall they know sorrow.

Echo Verse 10 from surah Saba

34:10 And We certainly gave David from Us bounty. [We said], "O mountains, repeat [Our] praises with him, and the birds [as well]." And We made pliable for him iron,

Be with Allah, and He will be with you. Do not ask when, how, or where. For the One who softened iron for David, peace be upon him, will find no difficulty in softening hearts for you.

The One who made the mountains and birds echo His praises will not find it hard to make you beloved among people.

Worship Him in obedience, and He promises you success. Offer Allah what He loves, and He will grant you what you desire. Trust in His wisdom, and He will unfold for you blessings beyond what you can imagine.

Echo Verse 9 from surah Al-Qasas

28:9 And the wife of Pharaoh said, "[He will be] a comfort of the eye for me and for you. Do not kill him; perhaps he may benefit us, or we may adopt him as a son." And they perceived not.

Consider Pharaoh, who slaughtered thousands of children before the birth of Moses, fearing the prophecy that a child from the Israelites would lead to the downfall of his reign. Yet, by divine wisdom, Pharaoh's heart was softened toward Moses; the very child he feared; and he raised him in his own palace.

What Allah has decreed will always come to pass, no matter the effort made to resist it. Indeed, the world is a place of causes, and we act upon those causes as part of Allah's decree. But our certainty rests not in the cause itself, but in the One who ordains it.

Echo Verse 7 from surah Maryam

19:7 (Allah said) "O Zakariya (Zachariah)! Verily, We give you the glad tidings of a son, His name will be Yahya (John). We have given that name to none before (him)."

His bones were weakened, gray hair ablaze,

His wife was old, barren in life's maze.

Yet he knew well, reasons rule mankind,

But Allah, the Almighty, is unconfined.

So, he raised his hands, with hope in his heart,

Prayed to the One who can never depart.

And the answer came, like light in the night,

For Allah's power is endless, His mercy bright.

Whoever clings to reasons alone,

Will be left to them; will be left alone.

But whoever clings to Allah, trusting His way,

He will guide the reasons, making night into day.

So, trust in the Lord, beyond all you see,

For reasons are nothing when Allah's decree.

Messages from Quran   *Dr. Ashi Ezz*

Echo Verse 34 from surah Luqman

31:34 Indeed, Allah [alone] has knowledge of the Hour and sends down the rain and knows what is in the wombs. And no soul perceives what it will earn tomorrow, and no soul perceives in what land it will die. Indeed, Allah is Knowing and Acquainted.

Do not dwell in worry for the days yet to come;
Instead, seek the pleasure of Allah, and let your heart be numb
To anxieties that cloud your path. For the future lies
In His hands alone, where His wisdom never dies.

Remember, your sustenance will not be claimed by another,
But your worship must flourish, like a seed from its mother.
Allah, the Almighty, has promised what you need,
Yet He calls you to strive, to plant the righteous seed.

Work diligently, and trust in His decree,
For in seeking His pleasure, your soul shall be free.

Endurance through Testing (Balaa)

Theme: Life's trials are tests of resilience and faith.

Key Verse: *"Do people think that they will be left to say, 'We believe' and they will not be tried?"* (Surah Al-Ankabut 29:2)

Echo Verse 17 from surah Ar-Rad

13:17 Thus Allah presents [the example of] truth and falsehood. As for the foam, it vanishes, [being] cast off; but as for that which benefits the people, it remains on the earth. Thus does Allah present examples.

There comes a moment, quiet yet loud,
When the righteous feel lost in the crowd.
They start to question the path they've known,
As if their truth is overthrown.

The boldness of falsehood, so loud and clear,
Speaks with a confidence that stirs up fear.
And those who stand for what is right,
Feel their grip on certainty slip from sight.

But doubt not, though the world may sneer,
The light of truth will soon appear.
Stand firm in the storm, for what is right,
And trust that dawn will break the night.

Echo Verse 20 from surah Yusuf

12:20 And they sold him for a reduced price - a few dirhams - and they were, concerning him, of those content with little.

Among the ascetics lies a world where: Joseph is sold, Noah is mocked,

Abraham is cast into the fire,

Moses is accused of sorcery,

The dowry of a prostitute is the head of Zakariya,

And Muhammad, peace be upon him, is stoned.

These are among the beloved of the Divine; what more proof do you need that this life is but temporary?

God bestows the loftiest honor upon those who bear the weight of trials with grace.

Through storms of hardship and waves of tribulation, they rise, earning a place of distinction known only to the steadfast.

In their endurance lies a radiant reward, for the Divine exalts those who persevere, crowning their struggles with eternal favor

Echo Verse 17 from surah Luqman

31:17 O my son, establish prayer, enjoin what is right, forbid what is wrong, and be patient over what befalls you. Indeed, [all] that is of the matters [requiring] determination.

In this world, we walk according to the destiny set by Allah Almighty. The illness that struck you could never have been avoided, and the death that claimed your loved one was inevitable, no matter how hard you tried to prevent it. The job you lost would have slipped away even if you polished your manager's shoes every morning.

The Prophet, may Allah bless him and grant him peace, how he has taught us to accept fate with grace. Know in your hearts that what befalls you was never meant to miss you, and what misses you was never meant to befall you.

Al-Hasan Al-Basri once said: "If we were only rewarded for what we desire, our reward would be little. But Allah is generous. He tests His servants with trials they do not choose, so that He may bestow upon them a greater reward."

Echo Verse 153 from surah Al Imran

3:153 [Remember] when you [fled and] climbed [the mountain] without looking aside at anyone while the Messenger was calling you from behind. **So, Allah repaid you with distress upon distress so you would not grieve** for that which had escaped you [of victory and spoils of war] or [for] that which had befallen you [of injury and death]. And Allah is [fully] Acquainted with what you do.

In grief, He brings you to your knees,
Through loss, He reveals your solitude,
Disappointment descends, a gentle whisper,
Reminding you that He is your steadfast shield.

In concealment, He teaches you the truth;
No one else can elevate your spirit,
In every stumble, He offers His embrace,
For no one else can guard your heart.

Misfortunes are not always vengeance's hand;
Many serve as lessons, guiding your way,
Discipline unfolds in the trials you face,
Correcting your course, steering you home.

Resilience Through Patience (Sabr)

Theme: Enduring difficulties with patience is one of the most frequently mentioned aspects of resilience in the Quran.

Key Verse: *"O you who have believed, seek help through patience and prayer. Indeed, Allah is with the patient."* (Surah Al-Baqarah 2:153)

Echo Verse 45 from surah Al-Baqarah

2:45 And seek help through patience and prayer, and indeed, it is difficult except for the humbly submissive [to Allah]

This world is a house of testing, not of reward,

Where calamities rain by the will of the Lord.

Loved ones lost, homes in despair,

Bad neighbors who make life unfair.

Do you not know? Our Prophet saw it all,

Faced every hardship, yet he stood tall.

So patient hearts pass the test with grace,

While angered souls fail and lose their place.

No soul is spared from life's affliction,

Not even prophets escaped this condition.

Messages from Quran   *Dr. Ashi Ezz*

For they were tested, the most of all,
Yet they rose through every fall.
So, be patient, be prayer and hold on tight,
For the reward comes after the longest night.

Echo Verse 111 from surah Al-Muminun

23:111 Indeed, I have rewarded them this Day for their patient endurance - that they are the attainers [of success]."

Patience, a virtue of the true winners, unfolds in countless forms.

Patience in shunning what is wrong,

Patience in staying steadfast and strong,

Patience when trials come along,

In God's decree, we belong.

In the realm of abstinence from sin, it is the restraint that holds power.

Be patient in abstaining, just as Allah, the Most High, elevates those who endure.

When desires call and you could easily succumb, yet you lower your gaze in the face of temptation; this is strength.

When a bribe lies before you, easy to take with no scandal in sight, but you refrain; that is integrity, patience in abstaining from sin, rewarded by Allah beyond measure.

And then, there is the patience in obedience.

When you give in charity, though your instinct craves wealth; when you rise for the dawn prayer, though the comfort of sleep pulls you back; when you walk to honor your parents, though the weight of life's demands bears down on you; this too is a sacred patience.

It is the endurance in devotion, the persistence in righteousness.

For every act of obedience, for every moment you choose the divine over the fleeting, the reward with Allah is vast, eternal, and profound.

Echo Verse 37 from surah Al-Anbiya

21:37 Man was created of haste. I will show you My signs, so do not impatiently urge Me.

This is the essence of our creation. We cannot rush to adulthood, expecting to resemble those children who, when promised something, ask about it every minute. Instead, we must temper that impatience with patience.

Many desires go unfulfilled because of haste. Al-Dhahabi narrates in A`lam al-Nubala' the story of Jaafar bin Abi Othman, who recounted a time at Yahya bin Ma'in's side when a man rushed in, exclaiming, "O Abu Zakariya, tell me something to remember!"

To which Yahya replied, "Remind me that you asked me to speak, yet I did not oblige." His message was clear: knowledge is not bestowed upon those who hurry. So let us learn the virtue of patience, for true wisdom flourishes in the soil of calm deliberation.

Echo Verse 18 from surah Yusuf

*12:18 And they brought upon his shirt false blood. [Jacob] said, "Rather, your souls have enticed you to something, **so patience is most fitting.** And Allah is the one sought for help against that which you describe."*

Patience is a beauty. Seek the Divine help for what you bear.

Peace to those who don't take all things to heart, who don't weep at every fall or pause at each word spoken.

They carry their own faults, never pinning blame on another's shame.

They see the world for what it is; shadowed and clear, knowing that evil walks with good, each a part of the whole.

They believe this life is but a passage, and that trusting in Allah is the surest way to cross it.

Be patient, my friend,
Hold fast to your Qur'an, let its wisdom guide your heart.
Embrace your prayers; let them be your solace.
Nurture your pain, for it is but a thread in Allah's grand tapestry,
A reminder that this world is but a fleeting test,
A mere transit station on our journey to the eternal.

Rest assured, we shall overcome,
And one day, in the embrace of Paradise,
We will look back with a gentle smile,
Laughing at the fleeting nonsense of this life,
Knowing we have triumphed over all.

Resilience Through Perseverance (Mujahada)

Theme: Struggling and persevering for the sake of Allah is a central part of resilience.

Key Verse: *"And those who strive for Us - We will surely guide them to Our ways. And indeed, Allah is with the doers of good."* (Surah Al-Ankabut 29:69)

Echo Verse 114 from surah Hud

11:114 And establish prayer at the two ends of the day and at the approach of the night. Indeed, good deeds do away with misdeeds. That is a reminder for those who remember.

Whenever you falter, remind yourself, "I lost a battle, but not the war." Do not despair; cleanse yourself with ablution, and pray two rak'ahs more.

Seek forgiveness for the fingers that strayed, and read the Qur'an with the same eyes that disobeyed.

"The repentant groans before Allah," a sound so sincere, For He is the Forgiving, always drawing you near.

He calls you back, with mercy so vast, to return to His embrace, where true peace will last.

Echo Verse 52 from surah Ta-Ha

20:52 [Moses] said, "The knowledge thereof is with my Lord in a record. My Lord neither errs nor forgets."

Allah does not forget. Not the thoughts you wrestled with, nor the tears you quietly dried. He remembers the sadness you lifted, the burdens you carried in silence.

Your tears, seen and heard, rise with prayers uttered in certainty.

He will not forget the times you withheld vengeance, though your hand could have returned the insult, nor the times you stepped away from battles destined to be a loss for everyone.

Your patience in the storm, your strength in the trial; these are never forgotten.

Even when the world fails to see your grace, do not despair. Allah knows who you are.

Echo Verse 22 from surah Az-Zumar

39:22 So is one whose breast Allah has expanded to [accept] Islam and he is upon a light from his Lord [like one whose heart rejects it]? Then woe to those whose hearts are hardened against the remembrance of Allah. Those are in manifest error.

Woe to the hardened hearts, oblivious even in the remembrance of the Divine.

You witness the sinner, arrogant in his delusion, who dares ask, "Why has Allah not punished me?" Foolish one, what punishment could be more severe than what you already endure?

A funeral procession passes, yet you remain unmoved.

You hear verses of death, but they do not stir your soul. You see the poor, yet your heart feels no compassion.

And still, you ask, "Where is the punishment?"

What torment is harsher than a heart turned into a graveyard? As Ibn al-Qayyim said, no punishment afflicts a servant greater than a heart grown cold and cruel.

Echo Verse 35 from surah Al-Baqarah

2:35 And We said, "O Adam, dwell, you and your wife, in Paradise and eat therefrom in [ease and] abundance from wherever you will. But do not approach this tree, lest you be among the wrongdoers."

Behold His mercy, when He forbade one tree, yet opened all of Paradise in grace. Satan, ever cunning, made the forbidden shine bright, though that tree held no special sight. He struck Adam's desire, promising immortality.

In Paradise, Allah ensured no hunger, no strife, but on Earth, we face toil and pain. Abundance surrounds, yet Satan narrows our vision. Usury, alcohol, pork; all forbidden, yet lawful paths remain, while Satan lures with delusion.

Adultery was banned, marriage made pure, But Satan never tires, making sin seem secure.
And so, cast from Paradise, we now stand on Earth's ground,
Two trains before us, one Hell-bound, one Heaven-bound.
The choice is ours, as clear as the light of day;
Which train, O soul, will take you away?

Echo Verse 56 from surah An-Naml

27:56 But the answer of his people was not except that they said, "Expel the family of Lot from your city. Indeed, they are people who keep themselves pure."

For thousands of years, corrupt societies have followed the same pattern: condemning the righteous for their virtues.

Sad but true; there comes a moment for the people of truth when they think they are insane, due to the audacity and confidence with which the people of falsehood speak.

Can you see it? they reproached Lot and his family for their purity. The corrupt stifle the good because they are a reminder of their own failings. The adulterer wishes all women sinned, the thief that all men stole, the bribed that everyone accepted bribes; So, their own guilt might fade.

They drag others down, accusing them of flaws they secretly envy. Don't believe them when they call modesty repression or truthfulness naïve. They hide their shame behind these words, knowing deep down they've lost their dignity.

So, do not change. Stand firm.

Forgive One Anther (Afw)

Theme: Letting go of grudges and forgiving others helps build emotional resilience and peace.

Key Verse: *"But if you pardon and overlook and forgive - then indeed, Allah is Forgiving and Merciful."* (Surah At-Taghabun 64:14)

Echo Verse 34 from Surah Fussilat

"And not equal are the good deed and the bad. Repel [evil] by that [deed] which is better; and thereupon the one whom between you and him is enmity [will become] as though he was a devoted friend."

Forgiveness, in its purest form, is an act of resilience, a testament to emotional fortitude, patience, and unwavering trust in Allah's justice.

In Islam, it is more than just compassion; it is a powerful declaration of inner strength.

To forgive is to rise above the wounds of the heart, to let go of personal grievances, and to focus on the higher aim of spiritual purity.

Through forgiveness, we release ourselves from the chains of anger and resentment, opening the door to inner peace and deeper resilience.

The life of the Prophet Muhammad (PBUH) shines as one of the greatest examples of this profound resilience through forgiveness. After years of persecution and hostility from the people of Mecca, he returned not with vengeance, but with victory in the form of mercy. Standing before his former oppressors, he declared, "Go, you are free."

This sweeping act of forgiveness was more than a gesture; it was a testament to his unmatched strength, humility, and deep commitment to unity. He transcended personal pain for the sake of a greater cause, fulfilling Allah's will with grace.

Equally moving is the Prophet's (PBUH) encounter with the people of Ta'if. Humiliated, rejected, and physically attacked by the town's people, he was given the chance to call for their destruction. Yet, instead of revenge, he prayed for their guidance.

In this moment, his resilience was not just in bearing the pain but in holding a hopeful vision for the future.

Through forgiveness, he taught us that true strength lies not in retribution, but in compassion and trust in Allah's plan.

Steadfastness (Istiqama)

Theme: Remaining firm in faith, even in the face of difficulties.

Key Verse: *"So remain on a right course as you have been commanded, [you] and those who have turned back with you [to Allah]."* (Surah Hud 11:112)

Echo Verse 21 from surah Al-Araf

7:21 And he swore [by Allah] to them, "Indeed, I am to you from among the sincere advisors."

Adam, our father, never thought anyone would dare to swear falsely by Allah, but Satan did not care. He twisted the truth, called things by other names, Tempting Adam with deceitful games.

The tree of disobedience, he called the tree of life, and in Satan's footsteps, devils continue their strife. Wine is now a spiritual drink, nudity is fashion, Obscenity is culture, adultery is openness, a misguided passion.

Do not be deceived by names, no matter how they change, For the essence of truth remains within range. Stay steadfast in faith, let wisdom be your guide, In the light of Allah, let your heart reside.

Echo Verse 63 from surah Al-Ankabut

29:63 And if you asked them, "Who sends down rain from the sky and gives life thereby to the earth after its lifelessness?" they would surely say " Allah." Say, "Praise to Allah "; but most of them do not reason.

If you reflect on how our Lord describes most people in the Qur'an, you'll find recurring themes: they do not know, they are not thankful, they do not understand. Yet, our Lord also describes, "But few are those who are thankful."

As has been passed down, Imam Ahmad once asked Hatim Al-Asam, "How does one find peace among people?"

Hatim replied, "You give them your wealth without taking from theirs. They may harm you, but you don't harm them. You prioritize their interests over your own."

Imam Ahmad responded, "This sounds hard and impractical." Hatim answered, "It is difficult, indeed. But more than that; it is nearly impossible."

So do not be swayed by the sheer number of wrongdoers. They may be many, but the truth is not in their numbers.

Echo Verse 14 from surah Al-Kahf

18:14 And We made firm their hearts when they stood up and said, "Our Lord is the Lord of the heavens and the earth. Never will we invoke besides Him any deity. We would have certainly spoken, then, an excessive transgression.

In this verse Allah is telling us about the Youth of the Cave. Hearts may waver, but it is Allah who grants steadfastness. No matter how deep your faith, never cease to seek firmness in your heart. Even the Prophet, the best of creation, would often call upon Allah, saying, "O Turner of hearts, make my heart firm upon Your religion."

Were it not for Allah's guidance holding firm the hearts of His servants, the devils would have led them astray. And yet, when His command came, the youth of the cave clung to the truth, while their entire city bowed to idols. Allah bound their hearts, and with that, the path became clear and easy.

Remember the mother of Moses, peace be upon him. As she placed him into the river, her heart might have shattered with grief, but Allah strengthened it. Without His mercy, she could not have done so.

Therefore, ask always for steadfastness, for Allah alone holds the power to bind hearts, to strengthen them, and to guide them upon His path.

Echo Verse 49 from surah Al-Kahf

18:49 And the record [of deeds] will be placed [open], and you will see the criminals fearful of that within it, and they will say, "Oh, woe to us! What is this book that leaves nothing small or great except that it has enumerated it?" And they will find what they did present [before them]. And your Lord does injustice to no one.

Your life is a book, and one day, in the hands of Allah, you will read its pages on the Day of Resurrection. So, be mindful not to be a poor author. Write today what you will not be ashamed to read tomorrow, while your book is still in your grasp and the eraser of forgiveness is within your reach.

Erase the stains of sin, and in the blank spaces, inscribe lines of light. rewrite your story; fill pages with charities, sentences of good deeds, a chapter of night prayers, and a pause of voluntary fasting.

Indeed, no one enters Paradise by their deeds alone; not even the Prophet, peace and blessings be upon him, for he too will enter by Allah's mercy. Yet, it is the good deeds that lead us to His boundless mercy, exalted is He.

Hope and Optimism (Husn al-Dhann)

Theme: Believing in the relief that follows hardship fosters resilience.

Key Verse: *"For indeed, with hardship [will be] ease. Indeed, with hardship [will be] ease."* (Surah Ash-Sharh 94:5-6)

Echo Verse 9 from surah Al-Qasas

28:9 And the wife of Pharaoh said, "[He will be] a comfort of the eye for me and for you. Do not kill him; perhaps he may benefit us, or we may adopt him as a son." And they perceived not.

This is what Asiya bint Muzahim said to her husband Pharaoh on the authority of Moses, peace be upon him,

Pharaoh replied, "He will be yours, but I have no need for him."

Reflecting on this moment, the Prophet, may Allah's peace and blessings be upon him, explained: "By the One in whose hand is my soul, had Pharaoh accepted his wife's words fully, without excluding himself, Allah would have guided him just as He guided her.

But Allah decreed otherwise for him.

Pharaoh was given reason and choice, yet he was denied that destiny.

So, always be optimistic, and speak the good or just stop and you will find goodness in return.

Trust in Allah's plan, for your destiny often reflects the words of your tongue and the outlook of your heart.

Resilience through Community (Ummah)

Theme: The collective strength of the community builds individual and societal resilience.

Verse: *"And cooperate in righteousness and piety, but do not cooperate in sin and aggression."* (Surah Al-Ma'idah 5:2)

Echo Verse 24 from surah Maryam

19:24 But he called her from below her, "Do not grieve; your Lord has provided beneath you a stream.

If ever there was one who could rise above the need for comfort in the darkest of times, it would have been Mary, the steadfast virgin.

Her unwavering faith could have made her the richest of souls. Yet, we are all but human, fragile in our moments of despair, in need of a tender hand to soothe our hearts.

So, when you find someone, whose flame has dimmed, touch their heart gently. Whisper kindness until their mind rekindles, glowing with life once more.

Look to Abu Bakr, the best of men after the prophets, lofty in faith. Even he, in the cave, found solace as the Prophet, peace be upon him, calmed his spirit with words: "O Abu Bakr, what do you think of two when Allah is their third?" And again, "Do not grieve, for Allah is with us."

The Prophet himself, peace be upon him, felt the weight of sorrow when Khadija, his beloved, and his uncle, Abu Talib, passed away.

Allah, knowing the depth of his heartache, gifted him with the miraculous journey of Isra and Mi'raj, lifting him beyond the earthly realm to console his soul.

For there are moments when the world feels unbearably tight, and no earthly comfort seems sufficient.

Yet, in these moments, seek out those who can guide you to the divine grace that provides the solace we cannot find elsewhere.

Echo Verse 76 from surah Ya-Sin

*36:76 So let not their speech grieve you.
Indeed, We know what they conceal and
what they declare.*

---

*Do not be saddened by their words,
for they will say of you what you are not.*

*Learn solace in those who came before you,
even though they are better than you.*

*Remember, they said of the Prophet;
may Allah bless him and grant him peace;
that he was a sorcerer, a madman, a liar.*

*They accused Joseph, peace be upon him, of theft,
and they slandered the Virgin Mary with adultery.*

*Hold this truth close: no one escapes
the tongues of people,
no matter how righteous or adorned in grace.*

Echo Verse 45 from surah Maryam

19:45 O my father, indeed I fear that there will touch you a punishment from the Most Merciful so you would be to Satan a companion [in Hellfire]."

The most exquisite form of love is the gentle urge to obey your Lord.

Those who disregard your afterlife, truly, they do not care for you.

If you witness a friend ensnared in sin and remain silent, know that your love for him is but a shadow, incomplete.

Do you fear to bruise his feelings while the flames of hell loom near?

Extend your hands to lead your loved ones toward Paradise.

Praise those who tread the path of obedience, and for those lost in disobedience, guide them back to Allah, even if it takes a firm grip upon their necks.

Omar bin Abdul Aziz once implored his friend:

"If you see me stray, seize my garments, shake me, and with urgency, remind me, 'O Omar, fear Allah, for the certainty of death is upon us all.

Echo Verse 71 from surah Al-Kahf

18:71 So they set out, until when they had embarked on the ship, al-Khidhr tore it open. [Moses] said, "Have you torn it open to drown its people? You have certainly done a grave thing."

Al-Khidr was not the sole hero of the tale; Moses, peace be upon him, stood as a hero in his own right.

When he rebuked Al-Khidr for breaching the ship, it seemed, at first glance, an act of aggression.

Likewise, when he denied the unjust killing of the boy, the situation appeared a clear crime.

Yet, he emerged as a man of noble principles, one who would not turn a blind eye to what he deemed false, refusing to favor Al-Khidr despite having journeyed far and wide to seek wisdom from him.

Echo Verse 40 from surah At-Tawbah

9:40 **"Do not grieve; indeed, Allah is with us."** *And Allah sent down his tranquility upon him and supported him with angels you did not see and made the word of those who disbelieved the lowest, while the word of Allah - that is the highest. And Allah is Exalted in Might and Wise.*

There are words much like hugs.

They enfold us, narrowing the space between us. At times, a gentle word from a friend arrives, expanding our minds, shattering old walls. At times, a tender touch from a lover soothes yet stirs the heart's quiet ache. And sometimes, a hug from someone dear lifts our spirits, lighting the darkness within.

We are but passing guests in this world, so let us soften the path for one another.

Endurance in the Face of Loss

Theme: Coping with loss while maintaining faith in Allah's wisdom.

Key Verse: *"And We will surely test you with something of fear and hunger and a loss of wealth and lives and fruits, but give good tidings to the patient."* (Surah Al-Baqarah 2:155)

Echo Verse 11 from surah An-Nur

24:11 Indeed, those who came with falsehood are a group among you. Do not think it bad for you; rather it is good for you. For every person among them is what [punishment] he has earned from the sin, and he who took upon himself the greater portion thereof - for him is a great punishment.

May Allah continue to act in ways beyond our understanding, for even within our trials, goodness waits to be unveiled. Reflect upon Surah Al-Kahf:

The ship, if it had not been pierced, would have been seized by the king, leaving the poor without their means of livelihood.

The boy whose life was taken; had he lived, he would have brought sorrow to his parents.

The wall of orphans, mended without charge, stood firm to protect their rights from being forsaken.

Trust in Allah, for the Lord of goodness brings forth only good.

In every hardship lies a concealed mercy, guiding us toward a greater wisdom that we have yet to grasp.

Echo Verse 12 from surah Al-Qasas

28:12 And We had prevented from him [all] wet nurses before, so she said, "Shall I direct you to a household that will be responsible for him for you while they are to him [for his upbringing] sincere?"

Before Moses felt the pangs of hunger, peace be upon him.
His cries echoed through Pharaoh's palace, stirring pity in every heart.
Yet, it was Allah, in His infinite mercy,
Who decreed that he should not nurse, for His wisdom was profound.
He sought to guide him back to the warmth of his mother.
If only we could perceive Allah's mercy in every deprivation,
And recognize His wisdom in every prohibition,
The path ahead would surely unfold with ease for us.

Just trust the Divine Wisdom

Lessons from the Prophets

Theme: The stories of the prophets, like Musa (Moses), Ayyub (Job), and Yusuf (Joseph), show immense resilience.

Key Verse: *"And We certainly sent into every nation a messenger, [saying], 'Worship Allah and avoid Taghut.'"* (Surah An-Nahl 16:36)

Echo Verse 90 from surah Al-Anam

6:90 Those are the ones whom Allah has guided, so from their guidance take an example. Say, "I ask of you for this message no payment. It is not but a reminder for the worlds."

Oh Allah, I do not pray as befits Your grandeur, Nor do I fast with the devotion of David's fervor.

I lack the patience of Job in his trials so severe, Nor do I praise You like Jonah in the whale's sphere.

I do not embrace my faith with Yahya's might, Nor lower my gaze like Joseph, pure and bright.

I am not as forgiving as Muhammad, our beloved guide, Who said, "Go, you are free," with mercy so wide.

But in my heart, Oh Allah, I strive to be true, for like them, Oh Allah, I deeply love You.

Echo Verse 5 from surah Yusuf

12:5 He said, "O my son, do not relate your vision to your brothers or they will contrive against you a plan. Indeed Satan, to man, is a manifest enemy.

Do not speak of every blessing Allah has granted you, especially not in front of all. Some souls are afflicted with sickness, and some eyes are tainted with poison. Be a fortress for Allah's gifts, safeguarding them with gratitude and secrecy. If you must speak, let it not be to everyone.

Envy is never satisfied until the grace it covets vanishes entirely. Remember, even Yusuf's brothers envied their own over a mere dream seen in sleep. So, do you expect to be safe from envy over your job, your spouse, your wealth, or your status? Guard what is precious, for not every heart rejoices in your joy.

Echo Verse 97 from surah Al-Hijr

15:97 And We already know that your chest is constrained by what they say.

*Hurtful words wound his spirit, igniting the flame of pain.
For even a prophet, a beacon of light, can feel the sting of disdain.
What then of those who tread below him?
May peace be upon those who select their words
As carefully as they choose their attire,
For they understand that speech is a form of elegance, a reflection of grace.*

Echo Verse 40 from surah Hud

11:40 [So it was], until when Our command came and the oven overflowed, We said, "Load upon the ship of each [creature] two mates and your family, except those about whom the word has preceded, and [include] whoever has believed." But none had believed with him, except a few.

He is the Sheikh of the Messengers; Noah, peace be upon him, who lived for a thousand years, not merely fifty. Yet, among his people, only a handful believed in his call.

We are responsible for the road we take, not for the outcome.

Our beloved Prophet foretold that on the Day of Resurrection, some prophets will stand before our Lord alone, having had no followers in their earthly lives.

Imam Al-Awza'i recalls, on the day that 'Ata' Ibn Abi Rabah passed, he was the most knowledgeable man on earth, yet only nine souls gathered to honor him. Such is the weight of knowledge; it is not measured by the multitude of followers, but by the truth it upholds and the steadfastness it inspires

---

Echo Verse 92 from surah Yusuf

12:92 He said, "No blame will there be upon you today. Allah will forgive you; and He is the most merciful of the merciful."

This is Joseph; they conspired to end his life but chose a lesser evil instead. They cast him into a dark pit, sold as one might sell a slave in the bustling markets.

Yet, when they become under his control, heads bowed in apology, he swiftly turned the page of the past.

Such is the nature of the noble: they let go of old wounds.

Prophet Muhammad embodied this grace; he embraced forgiveness wholeheartedly.

Let us follow the steps of our beloved Prophet

Echo Verse 37 from surah Al-Isra

17:37 And do not walk upon the earth exultantly. Indeed, you will never tear the earth [apart], and you will never reach the mountains in height.

Imam Ahmad once went down to the market in Baghdad, purchased a bundle of firewood, and carried it on his shoulder. When the people saw him, they rushed toward him. Shopkeepers left their stalls, and time seemed to pause as they greeted him. Everyone said, "Let us carry the firewood for you." His face flushed, and tears welled in his eyes. He humbly replied, "We are poor, and had it not been for Allah's protection, we would have been exposed."

Ahmad ibn Hanbal had learned humility from the Prophet, may Allah's prayers and peace be upon him. He knew well that the Prophet himself used to milk his sheep, mend his sandals, sew his clothes, race with his wife Aisha, and wipe the tears from Safiyah's eyes.

Once, when his companions were dividing tasks for slaughtering a sheep, one said, "I will slaughter it," and another said, "I will skin it." The Prophet, may Allah's prayers and peace be upon him, humbly added, "And I will collect the firewood."

Echo Verse 35 from surah Saad

38:35 He said, "My Lord, forgive me and grant me a kingdom such as will not belong to anyone after me. Indeed, You are the Bestower."

Solomon, peace be upon him, began his prayer with repentance and a plea for forgiveness, reflecting the deep wisdom of the prophets and their understanding of divine law. For it is often sin that stands as a barrier between a servant and the answer they seek from their Lord. One may ask, and ask again, yet find their supplication unmet; not because the request is unworthy, but because sin clings too closely, hindering divine mercy.

When the answer is delayed, pause, reflect, and examine the errors in which you may be entangled. It is these transgressions that hold back what you seek. Do not imagine that your request goes unanswered because it is too great; nothing is beyond Allah's power.

Look to Solomon, peace be upon him, who asked for the subjugation of the jinn, mastery over the winds, and the language of birds. All of this was granted to him by Allah. But before his asking, there was repentance; a cleansing of the soul, a return to humility, and only then did his heart open to receive the vast gifts bestowed.

Echo Verse 24 from surah Al-Qasas

28:24 So he watered [their flocks] for them; then he went back to the shade and said, "My Lord, indeed I am, for whatever good You would send down to me, in need."

When Moses, peace be upon him, arrived in Madyan, he had no home, no work, no place of refuge.

But after a small favor, went to the shade and lifted his hands to the heavens, saying: "O my Lord, from the goodness You bestow upon the needy, grant me my share."

The sun did not set that day before Moses had a house, a job, and a wife by his side.

So, after every good deed you do, try this prayer; May the Most Generous send his blessings upon you too.

Echo Verse 87 from surah Al-Anbiya

21:87 And [mention] the man of the fish, when he went off in anger and thought that We would not decree [anything] upon him. And he called out within the darknesses, "There is no deity except You; exalted are You. Indeed, I have been of the wrongdoers."

*It was never about candles,
nor lamps, nor lanterns.
It was always about the heart.*

The world could dim all its lights, extinguish every flame before your eyes; but what harm would that be if the glow within your chest still burned bright?

No sun nor moon, even perched upon your shoulder, could benefit you if your heart lay cloaked in shadow.

Look at Yunus, peace upon him, swallowed by threefold darkness: the night, the sea, the belly of the whale. Did those shadows harm him? No injustice clouded his heart, and so his trial was lightened.

A prophet, free of lies, protected from immorality and hypocrisy, when anger flared, it flared for Allah. And as he walked through the depths of the whale, he cried to his Lord:

*"There is no god but You. Glory be to You.
Indeed, I was of the wrongdoers."*

*He, infallible, knew his place with his Lord,
approaching Him in humility,
seeing his own faults even as a prophet.
How well Yunus humbled himself,
never boasting of obedience.*

*Yet, after two rak'ahs, we prayed, we stand as if
we've entered Paradise.
Such delusion.*

*Check your heart.
What use is a bright star in the sky, if the heart is
steeped in darkness?
And remember: every darkness outside is nothing
so long as the heart still holds its light.*

Echo Verse 69 from surah Al-Ahzab

33:69 O you who have believed, be not like those who abused Moses; then Allah cleared him of what they said. And he, in the sight of Allah, was distinguished.

Noah; they denied him. Abraham; they cast into the fire.

Moses; they sought to harm him, and Saleh; they tested with hardship.

Shu'ayb; they disobeyed, and Yahya; they unjustly killed.

Jesus; they attempted to crucify, and Muhammad; may Allah bless him and grant him peace; was rejected in Mecca,

challenged in Ta'if, and pursued on the path of migration.

At Uhud and Badr, they opposed him,

in the trench they besieged him, seeking to overwhelm.

So, what should you expect from people?

If you give in charity, they may question your motives.

If you hold back, they might think you're scared.

If you advise, some will listen, others may not.

If you remain silent, they may say he doesn't know.

Such are the people; among them are those who understand, and others who may not.

So be true to yourself, steadfast in your purpose,

for those who follow their path with sincerity find peace,

and those who remain patient find contentment.

Their approval comes and goes, but your integrity remains.

Seek, above all, the pleasure of Allah; for His recognition is everlasting,

and His guidance leads to a life of meaning and fulfillment.

Humility (Tawadu)

Theme: Humility allows individuals to accept challenges and mistakes, and helps them grow stronger.

Key Verse: *"And the servants of the Most Merciful are those who walk upon the earth easily, and when the ignorant address them [harshly], they say [words of] peace."* (Surah Al-Furqan 25:63)

Key Verse: *"And do not walk upon the earth with arrogance. Indeed, you will never tear the earth apart, and you will never reach the mountains in height."* (Surah Al-Isra 17:37)

Echo Verse 29 from surah An-Nahl

16:29 So enter the gates of Hell to abide eternally therein, and how wretched is the residence of the arrogant.

Hearts get sick just as bodies get sick, and treating body diseases is easier than treating diseases of the heart. And one of the deadliest diseases that afflict the heart is arrogance when a person sees that he is better than others because of money he was given, or a degree he obtained, or a job he held.

The Prophet taught us that, no one who has an atom's weight of arrogance in his heart will enter Paradise.

It was the habit of the righteous to immediately address any feeling of superiority they found. The great companion Abdullah bin Salam passed by the market carrying a bundle of firewood. It was said to him, "Hasn't Allah made you rich?" He said, "Yes, but." I wanted to suppress arrogance)

There's a vast difference between one who commits a sin while broken and one who does so while belittling it, arrogant. The one who sins and you advise, who says, "Pray for me, as my desires and whisperings of the devil have overcome me," is vastly different from the one who sins and says, "What is the problem? It is one life, enjoy it, man."

The first, his return to Allah, is easy, for his problem lies in his limbs. The second, his return to Allah, is difficult, for his problem lies in his heart.

Sufyan bin Uyaynah used to say: "Whoever's disobedience was in lust, he may still have some good in him. But whoever's disobedience was in pride, fear for him, for Adam, peace be upon him, disobeyed out of desire, and was forgiven. Satan, however, disobeyed arrogantly, and was cursed."

Echo Verse 24 from surah Al-Qasas

28:24 So he watered [their flocks] for them; then he went back to the shade and said, "My Lord, indeed I am, for whatever good You would send down to me, in need."

So, he provided them with water, then seek the shade.
Do not await the praise for each noble act,
Nor look for applause after every brave deed.
Live with a heart pure as freshly fallen snow.

Help those in need; console the weary souls.
Stand tall amidst the stumbling, be a pillar for the weak.
Make kindness your habit, as natural as breath.
When you give alms, do so with humble grace;
Let not your heart swell with pride, for you see,
The struggle of the poor unfolds before your eyes.

How noble was Moses, peace be upon him,
As he extended a hand in compassion,
And was met with gratitude as his reward.
Remember always, you are in the presence of the generous.

Echo Verse 6 from surah Al Imran

3:6 It is He who forms you in the wombs however He wills. There is no deity except Him, the Exalted in Might, the Wise.

In the intricate tapestry of existence, Allah has scattered beauty among His creations, reflecting resilience and the strength within us all. When we recognize and embrace our beauty; be it physical, emotional, or spiritual; we nurture a wellspring of resilience. Each person, enriched by beauty, gains the fortitude to face life's trials.

To those who feel lacking, remember: beauty exists on a vast spectrum, often rooted in the heart's capacity to love and endure. Just as Joseph epitomized beauty, we too can cultivate inner charm and strength amidst adversity. His story teaches us that while external beauty may attract, it is the inner strength that sustains us.

Reflecting on beauty can reignite our spirits, reminding us of our shared humanity and interconnectedness. Embrace your beauty and struggles, intertwining them to forge resilience. In this dance lies a profound truth: our capacity to endure and thrive is as boundless as the beauty surrounding us.

Self-Restraint (Taqwa)

Theme: Taqwa, or mindfulness of Allah, acts as a shield against temptation and helps one maintain resilience in the face of challenges.

Key Verse: *"And whoever fears Allah - He will make for him a way out."* (Surah At-Talaq 65:2)

Echo Verse 5 to 7 from surah Al-Layl

92:5 As for he who gives and fears Allah

92:6 And believes in the best [reward],

92:7 We will ease him toward ease.

As for the reason: the one who gives, who walks the path of piety.

And as for the result: we shall guide him gently into ease,

For when the world tastes sour to you, give from your wealth and your heart.

Feed the hungry, guide the lost, support the one who stumbles, and release the burden of debt.

Charity is not in coins alone;

It's in redressing thoughts, wiping away tears, mending broken hearts.

For nothing brings greater worry than sin,
And nothing soothes the soul more than obedience.
So, if your heart feels content, yet distracted;
Reflect on your worship and realign its course.

Echo Verse 28 from surah Al-Maidah

5:28 If you should raise your hand against me to kill me - I shall not raise my hand against you to kill you. Indeed, I fear Allah, Lord of the worlds.

I fear Allah, for in His presence, I find my peace.
The most beautiful apology, etched in the annals of time,
Came from Abel, a brother to Cain,
In the depths of conflict, a testament of grace.

Do not let the world sway you;
Hold fast to your faith, even if it costs you your life.
True, one can exist without religion,
But have you pondered what it means to live like beasts?

May Allah honor you with strength and clarity,
For He seeks in you the greatest pleasure,
The longest journey through this earthly existence.
Yet, in the end, all are destined to return to Him.

Courage in Adversity (Shuja'a)

Theme: Courage and bravery, especially in upholding the truth or defending one's faith, is a form of resilience.

Key Verse: *"But those who feared their Lord will be driven to Paradise in groups..."* (Surah Az-Zumar 39:73)

Echo Verse 67 from surah Ta-Ha

20:67 And he sensed within himself apprehension, did Moses.

Courage is not the absence of fear, but the ability to express it. We must remember, no matter how high someone stands, they are human. Moses feared the unknown, Abraham shared his vision with his son with trembling faith, and Jacob couldn't bear the loss of Joseph, saying, "It saddens me that you should take him." Even Muhammad, peace be upon him, wept at the death of his son, saying, "The heart grieves, the eyes weep, but we only say what pleases Allah."

No matter their greatness, they felt the same emotions; grief, joy, love, and anger. We all battle desires and dreams. The beggar finds joy in a kind word as much as a coin, the servant in gentle treatment, and the janitor in a smile. Rich or poor, all are human. The righteous are not just walking scriptures; laborers are not machines. We, people, are human; fragile, yet resilient.

Echo Verse 50 from surah Adh-Dhariyat

51:50 So flee to Allah. Indeed, I am to you from Him a clear warner.

Every escape is the refuge of the coward, but fleeing to Allah is the choice of the brave.

It is the flight of the victor, not that of the defeated, a decision made by the strong, not the weak.

In this realm of heroism, abstaining from sin while temptation beckons is a true act of valor. Returning humbled after straying; This too is a form of heroism, As is rising for the dawn prayer with courage anew.

Heroism is not confined to physical might. Remember the day when Abdullah bin Masoud climbed a tree, and laughter echoed at the sight of his legs.
Yet the Prophet, may Allah bless him and grant him peace, declared to them, "By the One in whose hand lies my soul,
Those legs weigh heavier on the scales
Than the mountain of Uhud."

Echo Verse 117 from surah At-Tawbah

9:117 Allah has already forgiven the Prophet and the Muhajireen and the Ansar who followed him in the hour of difficulty after the hearts of a party of them had almost inclined [to doubt], and then He forgave them. Indeed, He was to them Kind and Merciful.

The verse was revealed concerning the Companions during the Battle of Tabuk, one of the most challenging confrontations faced by the Prophet, may Allah bless him and grant him peace. This battle stretched over great distances, under the blazing summer sun, with the desert heat bearing down relentlessly. The army was aptly named the Army of Hardship, for resources were scarce, and many lacked the means to equip themselves.

Yet Allah, in His wisdom, reminds us that hardship is but a fleeting hour. Time flows swiftly, and days shift like the breeze. What remains of our obedience is its reward, and what lingers from our disobedience is its burden. In times of adversity, they found strength in one another, knowing that these days, too, shall pass. The promise that awaits them? Paradise, a reward for their unwavering faith.

Resilience in Leadership

Theme: Resilience is essential for leaders in facing societal challenges and guiding people through difficult times.

Key Verse: *"And We made from among them leaders guiding by Our command when they were patient and [when] they were certain of Our signs."* (Surah As-Sajdah 32:24)

Echo Verse 22 from surah Yusuf

12:22 And when Joseph reached maturity, We gave him judgment and knowledge. And thus We reward the doers of good.

There are matters in life that must ripen before you can reach them, for if you grasp them too soon, they will slip through your fingers.

The One who aided the Muslims at Badr could have granted them victory in Mecca while they were weak, but Lord delayed that triumph to first nurture their strength, so they might understand that the message they bear is far greater than the opposition they face.

It is the message of tawhid, for which the entire universe was created.

My dear, if we cracked the egg before the chick was fully formed, it would have perished.

If we harvested the wheat too soon, it would never become bread, nor could we eat it.

Food uncooked remains raw, unfit to nourish.

Everything has its appointed time, so do not rush; let the process unfold as it must.

Echo Verse 68 from surah Ta-Ha

20:68 Allah said, "Fear not. Indeed, it is you who are superior.

Falsehood may claim a battle,

But truth prevails in the war.

Nimrod once triumphed, but Abraham, peace upon him,

Rose in victory far greater.

Pharaoh seized a fleeting win,

Yet Moses, peace upon him, emerged to reign.

Muhammad, peace and blessings be upon him,

Left Mecca in the shroud of night,

Only to return, triumphant, at dawn,

Through its gates with daylight's might.

Let not the glimmer of falsehood sway,

For its fleeting gains deceive the eye.

Nor let your faith in truth waver,

Though its final victory has yet to rise.

Allah holds the reins on dew and time,

To expose the false and refine the true.

Messages from Quran — *Dr. Ashi Ezz*

Echo Verse 77 from surah Yusuf

12:77 They said, "If he steals - a brother of his has stolen before." **But Joseph kept it within himself and did not reveal it to them**.

Joseph kept it within himself, revealing nothing to them. Though it is true that reproach can cleanse the heart and heal the wound, not every moment calls for it. Healing, much like stitching a wound, requires the right timing.

Sometimes, you must feign ignorance even though you understand everything, and pretend not to see even when you've seen it all. In certain moments, neglecting a matter may seem like a temporary loss, but the wise know that winning hearts matters far more than winning arguments.

Joseph, peace be upon him, did not choose this path out of weakness but out of wisdom. Overlooking faults is a trait of the noble.

Imam Ahmad once said, "Nine-tenths of well-being lies in ignoring (missteps of others)"

Imam Al-Shafi'i echoed, "The prudent and wise are those who overlook missteps of others."

Ibn al-Qayyim taught, "Part of courage is ignoring the missteps of others."

Resilience Though Overcoming Despair (Ya's)

Theme: Avoiding despair and keeping hope alive even in difficult situations is key to resilience.

Key Verse: *"And who despairs of the mercy of his Lord except for those astray?"* (Surah Al-Hijr 15:56)

Echo Verse 5 from surah As-Sajdah

32:5 He arranges [each] matter from the heaven to the earth; then it will ascend to Him in a Day, the extent of which is a thousand years of those which you count.

He governs all matters, from heaven to earth. In this, do not worry; place your trust in Allah Almighty. The illness that has befallen you, the debt that weighs heavy upon your heart, the worries that suffocate your peace, and the distress that clouds your relief; all of it is known to Him.

Stay close to His door, for while the generous among people strive to fulfill the needs of others, how much more will Allah, the All-Sufficient, provide? Trust in Him, and let your heart find solace in His boundless mercy.

Echo Verse 286 from surah Al-Baqarah

2:286 Allah does not charge a soul except [with that within] its capacity.

Allah does not place fruit upon a branch that cannot bear its weight. Every responsibility He entrusts to you is a testament to your strength. In every battle your king has set before you, know that you are equipped to face it. Each loophole assigned to your watch is yours to guard, so hold it close, even amid worry and despair.

Grief may shadow your path, but remember: you are greater than your trials, capable of withstanding the storm. Difficulties and misfortunes serve only to fortify your spirit, so stand firm in your position. Let not the challenges deter you, for within you lie the strength to rise anew.

Echo Verse 87 from surah Yusuf

12:87 O my sons, go and find out about Joseph and his brother and despair not of relief from Allah. Indeed, no one despairs of relief from Allah except the disbelieving people."

"They say the best of worship is waiting for relief;
when everything around whispers there is no solution,
yet your heart knows the matter rests in the Divine's hands.

The world turns, events unfold, but they are mere reasons,
meant for creation, not for the Creator. Do not despair.

Jacob, peace be upon him, did not utter these words in ease;
he spoke them after losing Benjamin,
after the heartache of Joseph's loss.

Yet in days, he caught Joseph's scent on the breeze,
and soon after, held him close once more.

So trust in Allah, always.

Echo Verse 114 from surah Hud

11:114 And establish prayer at the two ends of the day and at the approach of the night. Indeed, good deeds do away with misdeeds. That is a reminder for those who remember.

When good deeds cleanse the bad, the math is simple: if you cannot banish disobedience, then surround it with obedience.

If your eyes stray to what is forbidden, purify them with ablution and offer prayer. Should your tongue slip into backbiting, redeem it with charity.

If Satan claims a victory, rise again, for a thousand acts of service stand ready to overturn his defeat.

Know this: the groaning of the sinner is dearer to Allah than the prayer of the self-assured.

The obedient may have grown distant from Satan's grasp, but the sinner fights on, embattled, broken by disobedience yet forcing himself back into obedience.

He stumbles into sin, yet reaches for worship; always broken, always returning.

And as you return to Allah in humility and shame, be at peace; you are, indeed, doing well.

Echo Verse 140 from surah Al Imran

3:140 If a wound should touch you - there has already touched the [opposing] people a wound similar to it. And these days [of varying conditions] We alternate among the people so that Allah may make evident those who believe and [may] take to Himself from among you martyrs - and Allah does not like the wrongdoers –

Days weave in and out among the people, like threads in a grand tapestry.

Who could have imagined that Moses, peace be upon him, once a humble shepherd tending flocks, would one day ascend to speak to the Divine?

Or that Muhammad, peace and blessings be upon him, who cared for the sheep of the Quraish for a mere pittance, would rise as the Seal of the Prophets and Messengers?

Perhaps the most beautiful days of your life have yet to unfold.

With a bit of effort and unwavering faith in Allah, you will witness that what lies ahead is destined to be even more splendid

Resilience Through Obedience to Allah
(Ita'at Allah)

Theme: Resilience comes from the strength derived from following Allah's commandments.

Key Verse: *"And whoever obeys Allah and His Messenger has certainly attained a great attainment."* (Surah Al-Ahzab 33:71)

Echo Verse 92 from surah At-Tawbah

9:92 Nor [is there blame] upon those who, when they came to you that you might give them mounts, you said, "I can find nothing for you to ride upon." They turned back while their eyes overflowed with tears out of grief that they could not find something to spend [for the cause of Allah].

Abu Laila and Abdullah bin Mughffal came to the Prophet, may Allah bless him and grant him peace, on the day of Tabuk, asking him to give each of them a horse to fight on so they could join the army.

When the Prophet told them that he had run out of horses, they went back, crying.

Imagine this, they just cried over the loss of obedience.

I wonder, how much they would be crying if they had committed a sin. This is the case of a true believer.

It is difficult for them to have the doors closed between them and an obedience that can get them closer to Allah.

They might also think they were distant from that because of a sin that they had done before.

These are your ancestors, be proud.

Echo Verse 60 from surah Al-Anbiya

21:60 They said, "We heard a young man mention them who is called Abraham."

To the people, Abraham (peace be upon him) appeared as just a young man.

However, to Allah, his faith was as strong as a whole Ummah.

Therefore Allah, in His boundless power, bent the very laws of creation for him.

Cast into the blazing fire, it became cool and tranquil by Allah's command.

His wife, Sarah, aged and frail, found her body renewed by divine will, and she bore Isaac, peace be upon him, in her twilight years.

When Pharaoh sought to claim Sarah, the king of kings stopped that from happening.

So, seek not your worth in the eyes of men, for your true value lies in your standing with Allah.

Moderation and Balance (Wasatiyyah)

Theme: Leading a balanced life in times of ease and difficulty builds resilience.

Key Verse: *"Thus We have made you a just community that you will be witnesses over the people..."* (Surah Al-Baqarah 2:143)

Echo Verse 95 from surah Maryam

19:95 And all of them are coming to Him on the Day of Resurrection alone.

Alone you will stand; stripped of the wealth you gathered, the prestige you wielded, and the family you cherished.

As it has been passed down through the wise ones; When Sultan Suleiman the Magnificent lay on his deathbed, he turned to those around him and said, "When I die, let my hand hang from the coffin," so that all might see; even the Sultan leaves this world empty-handed.

It is fine for one to strive in this life, to build and beautify one's home. But never forget the grave, for that too awaits you.

Work for your worldly life, but not at the expense of your afterlife, for in the end, only the deeds you carry will remain.

Echo Verse 34 from surah Al-Kahf

18:34 And he had fruit, so he said to his companion while he was conversing with him, "I am greater than you in wealth and mightier in [numbers of] men."

Allah grants the world to those who love Him and even to those who turn away, but religion is a gift reserved for the faithful.

Solomon, peace be upon him, received the earth's fullness, yet wealth also touched Dhul-Qarnayn, Qarun, and Nimrod.

If riches defined worth, they would not grace both prophet and tyrant alike.

The truly poor are those who hold only gold, believing they can purchase everything; even Paradise. They mistake worldly wealth for richness in the Hereafter.

But money is merely a wheel, not the end or the means of life.

When placed beneath our feet, it lifts us; held above our heads, it brings us low.

Wealth does not tarnish faith; rather, it flourishes in the hands of the righteous.

What matters is that money serves you, not the other way around.

Wealth may soften life's edges, yet the finest treasures are beyond its reach.

Money can buy medicine, but not health; a bed, but not restful sleep; a poem, but never love; a song, but not a lover; a desk, but not true knowledge.

Both rich and poor can only eat to their fill and wear one garment.

Use wealth so it may serve you.

Make it a slave, never a master.

Lead your life with grace, for the richest treasures are those that cannot be bought.

Patience in Justice (Adl)

Theme: Standing up for justice and being resilient in seeking it, even against personal interest, is a major aspect of resilience in Islam.

Key Verse: *"O you who have believed, be persistently standing firm in justice, witnesses for Allah, even if it be against yourselves..."* (Surah An-Nisa 4:135)

Echo Verse 8 from surah Al-Maidah

5:8 O you who have believed, be persistently standing firm for Allah, witnesses in justice, and do not let the hatred of a people prevent you from being just. Be just; that is nearer to righteousness. And fear Allah; indeed, Allah is Acquainted with what you do.

Intense hatred will destroy you, and intense love will destroy you.

Joseph, peace be upon him, was afflicted with both. As for intense hatred, it was the reason for his brothers casting him into the pit.

As for intense love, it was the reason for his imprisonment. Sometimes we are not in control of our hearts, but we are commanded to be just.

Whether we love it or hate it, let us not turn the bad deeds of the one we love into good deeds, nor turn the good deeds of the one we hate into bad deeds.

Be fair and put things in their right place.

Abdullah bin Muhammad Al-Warraq said: We came to Imam Ahmad, and he asked us, "Where have you been?"

We said, "From the gathering of Abu Kurayb,"

and he said, "Write about him. He is a righteous old man."

We said, "But he criticizes you."

He answered "He is righteous old man; he is simply afflicted with me."

Resilience in Family Ties (Silat Ar-Rahm)

Theme: Maintaining family ties and supporting loved ones, even when faced with challenges, is a significant aspect of resilience.

Key Verse: *"And fear Allah, through whom you ask one another, and the wombs (kinship). Indeed, Allah is ever, over you, an Observer."* (Surah An-Nisa 4:1)

Echo Verse 237 from surah Al-Baqarah

2:237 And if you divorce them before you have touched them and you have already specified for them an obligation, then [give] half of what you specified - unless they forego the right or the one in whose hand is the marriage contract foregoes it. And to forego it is nearer to righteousness. ***And do not forget graciousness between you.*** *Indeed Allah, of whatever you do, is Seeing.*

I shall not quarrel with you; I will not raise a sword against the one I once adored.
Do not treat our bond with such trivial disdain,
For I cherish the virtues that we still retain.

Yet, when our path reaches a dead-end,
And respect and trust begin to bend,
I rise in quietude, my heart in prayer,
Two rak'ahs I offer, in hope and care.

*"O Allah," I call, "unite our hearts as new, or
Replace him with someone better, and me with one
true."*

*Then I start with Salam; and wait and see with a
heart of grace;*

if no way,

*I surrender and depart, trusting in Allah wisdom
to guide each weary heart.*

Echo Verse 26 from surah Al-Qasas

28:26 One of the women said, "O my father, hire him. Indeed, the best one you can hire is the strong and the trustworthy."

From the great Prophet Moses, peace be upon him,
His mother, in trust, cast him into the river's flow.
Fear not for him, the call of destiny knows no bounds.
His second mother, the one who raised him from the waters,
Held him close, yet it was his first who gave him life.
"Do not slay him," the decree echoed in hearts unspoken,
And his sister watched over, walking in quiet shadows.
His wife, a companion in life, sealed his fate with a word:
"My father, hire him; he is strong and true."
Indeed, no great man rises without a woman's hand shaping his path.

Patience in the Face of Injustice

Theme: Resilience through enduring injustice with faith in Allah's ultimate justice.

Key Verse: *"And whoever is patient and forgives - indeed, that is of the matters [requiring] determination."* (Surah Ash-Shura 42:43)

Echo Verse 111 from surah Ta-Ha

20:111 And [all] faces will be humbled before the Ever-Living, the Sustainer of existence. And he will have failed who carries injustice.

Allah, the Almighty, abhors nothing more than injustice, save only polytheism.

From His hatred for injustice and the oppressors, He answers the supplications of the oppressed infidel against the oppressive Muslim.

This is not love for the infidel nor hatred for the Muslim, but love for justice and hatred for injustice.

Ibn Taymiyyah said: Allah grants victory to the just infidel state over the unjust Muslim state.

A man wrote to Abdullah bin Omar, "Write to me with all the knowledge."

Ibn Omar replied, "Knowledge is vast, but remember, one day you will face Allah. So, lighten your burden from the blood of the people, avoid consuming their wealth, and spare your tongue from their honor. Commit to the righteous doers, do good, and speak peace."

Echo Verse 10 from surah Al-Qamar

54:10 So he invoked his Lord, "Indeed, I am overpowered, so help."

This is Noah's supplication. Beware of the supplication of those who have none but Allah.

Take heed of the poor worker whose wages you have devoured, the weak wife whose inheritance you have disdained, the brother whose rights you have usurped, and the neighbor whose land you have invaded.

Perhaps while you slept soundly the night before, he rose in the stillness, performed his ablution, and called upon Allah with Noah's supplication, Peace be upon him.

In that moment, Allah Almighty received the cries of the oppressed and commanded His angels to support His servant.

It was passed through generations that Jaafar Al-Barmaki once asked his father while they languished in prison, "O my father, after all the command, the prohibition, and the wealth? How did we end up here?" His father replied, "O my son, remember the oppressed, for we have neglected them, but Allah has not forgotten."

Echo Verse 44 from surah Hud

11:44 And it was said, "O earth, swallow your water, and O sky, withhold [your rain]." And the water subsided, and the matter was accomplished, and the ship came to rest on the [mountain of] Judiyy. And it was said, "Away with the wrongdoing people."

The Quran's divine words, a beacon of light,
In the face of oppression, they guide us through night.

From echoes of history, rich lessons unfold,
Resilience ignites in despair's chilling hold.
As rain from the heavens caresses the bare,
Nurturing life, in its gentle embrace, we share.

From desolate sands, a vessel takes a trip,
Navigating the waves, transforming dark into light.
Within its strong hull, the hopes of the many,
In struggle and loss, a new strength we'll carry.

Though the past may cast shadows of pain,
Victory greets those who rise once again.
With faith as our anchor, we weather the strife,
Embracing the journey, reclaiming our life.

In this grand tapestry, each thread weaves a tale,
Of triumph and trials that teach us to prevail.
For those who confront every hurdle they face,
Resilience blooms in each step we embrace.

Messages from Quran   *Dr. Ashi Ezz*

Resilience Through Contentment (Rida)

Theme: Resilience through accepting and being content with what Allah has decreed, without resentment or frustration.

Key Verse: *"Say, 'Never will we be struck except by what Allah has decreed for us; He is our protector.' And upon Allah let the believers rely."* (Surah At-Tawbah 9:51)

Echo Verse 32 from surah Al-Qalam

68:32 Perhaps our Lord will substitute for us [one] better than it. Indeed, we are toward our Lord desirous."

Extinguish with this verse the fire of your sorrow, For every missed chance, and every lost tomorrow. For every job that slipped through your grasp, and every lover who let go of your hand's clasp.

For every friend who wore a beautiful face, but hid a predatory wolf in their embrace.

What Allah has taken from you, let it be, A sign of His wisdom, a path to set you free.

Trust in His plan, for He knows best, in every trial, find your heart's rest. For what is lost, He will replace, With something better, by His grace.

Echo Verse 22 from surah Al-Hadid

57:22 No disaster strikes upon the earth or among yourselves except that it is in a register before We bring it into being - indeed that, for Allah, is easy

57:23 In order that you not despair over what has eluded you and not exult [in pride] over what He has given you. And Allah does not like everyone self-deluded and boastful

I wonder why mankind still worries, even after knowing these words of truth.

The divine wisdom behind every event, in the world and in our lives, is clear.

Trials and blessings are no accident, but part of Allah's perfect plan, written long before they unfold.

In this, we find balance; never sinking into despair when hardships come, nor rising in arrogance when success is granted.

It teaches us to walk with humility, to wait with patience, and to trust fully in Allah's decree.

For every moment has a purpose, and for Allah, nothing is beyond His ease.

Echo Verse 97 from surah An-Nahl

16:97 Whoever does righteousness, whether male or female, while he is a believer - We will surely cause him to live a good life, and We will surely give them their reward [in the Hereafter] according to the best of what they used to do.

Saeed bin Jubayr once said, "A good life is one where Allah spares you the need for others." While this is a beautiful sentiment, the essence of a good life runs deeper. It's not merely the absence of illness or poverty, nor is it about holding prestige or power. True goodness lies in being content with Allah's decree, whatever it may be.

Dissatisfaction with Allah's plan brings only distress, fatigue, and hardship. But when Allah blesses you with contentment in every circumstance, enabling you to be grateful in times of prosperity and patient through trials, then indeed, you have been granted a truly good life.

Patience in Dawah (Calling to Faith)

Theme: Prophets demonstrated patience and resilience when calling people to the faith, despite constant rejection and hostility.

Key Verse: *"So be patient, [O Muhammad], as were those of determination among the messengers and do not be impatient for them..."* (Surah Al-Ahqaf 46:35)

Echo Verse 43 from surah Hud

11:43 [But] he said, "I will take refuge on a mountain to protect me from the water." [Noah] said, "There is no protector today from the decree of Allah, except for whom He gives mercy." And the waves came between them, and he was among the drowned.

He who was raised in the home of a prophet was swallowed by the flood (the son of Noah), while he who was raised in Pharaoh's palace (Moses) split the sea with his staff. It is not where you begin, but how you journey through.

What matters is not the house in which you dwell, but the heart with which you live. Not the start of your story, but the way it ends, for it is the ending that seals the worth of all that came before.

Echo Verse 125 from surah An-Nahl

16:125 Invite to the way of your Lord with wisdom and good instruction, and argue with them in a way that is best. Indeed, your Lord is most knowing of who has strayed from His way, and He is most knowing of who is [rightly] guided.

No matter how right you are and how wrong the other may be, no matter how firmly you stand on the path of guidance while they wander astray, remember: morals come first.

Once, a thief broke into the home of Malik Ibn Dinar, only to find nothing to steal. Malik called out to him, "You search for something in this world to take, but what about doing something for the afterlife?" The thief replied, "Yes, I would like to do." Malik then instructed him, "Perform ablution and pray two rak'ahs."

The thief obeyed, praying earnestly before sitting in reflection. After a while, he rose and made his way to the mosque. When asked about this man, Malik replied, "He came to steal from us, and in turn, we have stolen him." For in that moment of guidance, a heart was transformed, and the true treasure was found; not in possessions, but in the pursuit of righteousness.

Echo Verse 8 from surah As-Saff

61:8 They want to extinguish the light of Allah with their mouths, but Allah will perfect His light, although the disbelievers dislike it.

No, the Qur'an will be silence.

Nor the Athan and prayers will stop

The caravan of Islam will not stop. Whoever rode in it arrived and whoever left behind will get lost.

This faith will keep going as the night and day will reach.

Unstoppable, resilient, and eternal.

Echo Verse 46 from surah At-Tawbah

9:46 And if they had intended to go forth, they would have prepared for it [some] preparation. But Allah disliked their being sent, so He kept them back, and they were told, "Remain [behind] with those who remain."

When Allah chooses to use you in the service of His faith, He has gazed into your heart,
And found you a soul capable of aiding others.

Do not envy the renowned for their fleeting fame;
If Allah held them dear, He would guide them to His obedience.
And spare not a thought for the billionaires,
Whose wealth is devoid of good deeds;
For if Allah cherished them,
They would not be forsaken.

Resilience in Economic Hardship

Theme: Resilience isn't just about personal hardship but also includes surviving economic challenges while maintaining faith and integrity.

Key Verse: *"Who is it that would loan Allah a goodly loan so He may multiply it for him many times over?"* (Surah Al-Baqarah 2:245)

Echo Verse 1 from surah At-Talaq

65:1 And whoever transgresses the limits of Allah has certainly wronged himself. You know not; perhaps Allah will bring about after that a [different] matter.

When a person feels trapped, believing there is no way out, relief comes from Allah Almighty in ways unimaginable.

Who could have thought that Hagar, running between Safa and Marwah in search of water, would witness water burst forth at her son's feet? The Zamzam well was not only for him to drink but for entire nations to benefit from; until now and beyond.

In the blink of an eye, Allah transforms adversity into something fleeting. As Ibn al-Qayyim reminds us, we've all faced moments that felt like the end, yet today, they are merely memories. So, never despair. Trust in your Lord, for the greatest act of worship is patiently awaiting relief from Him.

Echo Verse 46 from surah Al-Kahf

18:46 Wealth and children are [but] adornment of the worldly life. But the enduring good deeds are better to your Lord for reward and better for [one's] hope.

The world may appear easier with wealth, and the joys of children often feel sweeter. Yet pause and reflect on this wisdom: money is but an adornment, not the true measure of one's worth. True value lies in knowledge, and nothing holds greater significance than knowing your Creator and submit to him.

Your worth is determined by the content of your heart, not the depth of your pockets. Real strength resides in kindness, not in authority, and in compassion, not in cruelty.

Do not envy those like Qarun for their riches; when the earth swallowed him and his grand estate, the truth was laid bare. You have known this truth long before; let it illuminate your heart and guide

Resilience Through Managing Fear

Theme: Overcoming fear and staying resilient during times of conflict, trials, and uncertainty is highlighted in the Quran.

Key Verse: *"It is only Shaytan that suggests to you the fear of his allies, so fear them not, but fear Me, if you are true believers."* (Surah Al-Imran 3:175)

Echo Verse 19 from surah Al-Inshiqaq

84:19 [That] you will surely experience state after state.

After distress, there comes relief; after illness, health; after sadness, joy; and after separation, a reunion. This world never stays the same; its seasons shift, and its states are fleeting. We are carried between poverty and wealth, health and sickness, sorrow and solace, farewells and reunions, moments of joy and trials of grief.

Yet, blessed is the one who remains with Allah through every change, steadfast in every condition, for with Him, every fluctuation of this life becomes a bridge to something greater; a promise of peace that endures beyond all passing storms.

Echo Verse 62 from surah Ash-Shuara

26:62 [Moses] said, "No! Indeed, with me is my Lord; He will guide me."

O Allah, grant me certainty like that of Moses,
When he stood before the sea, with Pharaoh in pursuit,
And his people cried, "We are caught."
But he replied, "No! Indeed, with me is my Lord; He will guide me."

They were guided, faith unwavering, in the face of fear.

O Allah, instill in me the certainty
Of the Prophet, peace and blessings be upon him,
When Abu Bakr trembled, whispering,
"If anyone looked beneath their feet,
They would see us." The Prophet, calm and resolute,
Replied, "O Abu Bakr, what do you think of two when Allah is the third with us?"

Echo Verse 85 from surah Maryam

19:85 On the Day We will gather the righteous to the Most Merciful as a delegation

---

Fear not if you miss the parades for this life kings,

For the true worth lies in one gathering;

The delegation destined for the King of Kings; the Almighty.

Where resilience finds its highest meaning,

In the presence of the Almighty, everlasting and supreme.

Echo Verse 5 from surah Al-Ankabut

29:5 Whoever should hope for the meeting with Allah - indeed, the term decreed by Allah is coming. And He is the Hearing, the Knowing.

The Lord dwells within the hearts of those who love Him, soothing their thoughts with a sweetness that transforms fear into peace.

To His beloved ones, He seems to whisper, "Nothing separates us but death." But this does not imply that faith demands a love of death over life.

The instinct to cherish life is universal, shared equally by believer and unbeliever.

When Aisha once asked the Messenger of Allah, peace and blessings be upon him, about the verse: "They hated meeting Allah, so Allah hated meeting them," she questioned, "Who loves death?" The Prophet responded, "This is not what is meant, Aisha." He explained that before a person's soul departs, they are shown their place in Paradise or Hell. For the disbeliever who sees his grim fate, a dread of meeting Allah arises, and Allah, in His wisdom, mirrors that aversion.

What a Book; concise yet profound; Its brevity carries oceans of meaning.

Trials as Purification (Tazkiyah)

Theme: Adversities are sometimes seen as a way to purify and elevate a person's soul, enhancing spiritual resilience.

Key Verse: *"Indeed, Allah has purchased from the believers their lives and their properties [in exchange] for that they will have Paradise. They fight in the cause of Allah, so they kill and are killed..."* (Surah At-Tawbah 9:111)

Echo Verse Surah Al-Ankabut (29:64)

And this worldly life is not but diversion and amusement. And indeed, the home of the Hereafter - that is the [eternal] life, if only they knew."

Imam Shafi'i once spoke words that still resonate deeply.

He said, "All people are dead, except those who seek knowledge.

And those with knowledge are asleep, except those who act upon it.

But even those who act are deceived, except the sincere.

And the truly sincere? They are never free from doubt, always questioning their sincerity, always worrying; until they step foot in Paradise."

The Prophet told us this world is the prison of the believer and the paradise of the non-believer.

Why a prison? Because here, you don't get to do as you please.

You're bound by the limits your Lord has set; by His commands and prohibitions.

If you seek freedom here, you'll find yourself enslaved in the hereafter.

But if you choose to be a servant of Allah in this life, Insha'Allah, you will be free in Paradise.

Echo Verse 25 from surah Al-Isra

17:25 Your Lord is most knowing of what is within yourselves. If you should be righteous [in intention] - then indeed He is ever, to the often returning [to Him], Forgiving.

Your Lord knows best what lies within your soul. If they speak of you in falsehood, if they wound your intentions or accuse you from the depths of their own darkness, if they taunt you with a glance or jab with malicious whispers; none of this can touch you. As long as Allah knows the truth in your words, their praises, no matter how abundant, will bring you no gain. Even if they adorn you with the garments of the pious and hold you among the few righteous, it will not avail you if Allah knows otherwise within your heart.

Remember, Allah does not gaze upon your outward form but peers into the essence of your heart. Tend to the place where the Creator looks, and let that be your peace. Then, keep going in the right path reassured.

Echo Verse 59 from surah Al-Anam

6:59 And with Him are the keys of the unseen; none knows them except Him. And He knows what is on the land and in the sea. Not a leaf falls but that He knows it. And no grain is there within the darknesses of the earth and no moist or dry [thing] but that it is [written] in a clear record.

How is that goodness dwelling in your heart? How is the love you carry for others, the joy you feel at their success, as if it were your own? And how do you share in their pain, as if it were your own suffering, too?

Remember, my friend, Allah does not gaze at us from above but looks deep within. So, tend well to the place where the King looks. For there is a piece of flesh in the body; if it is sound, the whole body is sound; but if it is corrupted, the entire body is corrupted. And that piece is the heart. Fix the heart, and all will follow.

Echo Verse 37 from surah Al-Ahzab

33:37 And you feared the people, while Allah has more right that you fear Him.

Stand firm for these:

Worship, before bending to customs.
Abandon what is forbidden, before yielding to shame.
Honor the halal, before submitting to worldly norms.
Embrace the Sunnah, before clinging to what feels familiar.
Place Allah above all, before seeking the approval of people.

Echo Verse 31 from surah Maryam

19:31 And He has made me blessed wherever I am and has enjoined upon me prayer and zakah as long as I remain alive

---

It is not important that you simply exist, but how you exist. True character is like pure metal; untouched by the passage of time. Wealth, status, and degrees should only deepen one's humility, for the wicked remain wicked, whether they polish shoes or sit as ministers.

When they spoke to Joseph, peace be upon him, they said, "We see you as one of the doers of good," both when he sat upon the king's throne and when he languished in prison. The noble heart remains noble, no matter where life places it, for it is not circumstance but character that defines a person's worth.

Echo Verse 12 from surah Al-Insan

76:12 And will reward them for what they patiently endured [with] a garden [in Paradise] and silk [garments].

The Fajr prayer demands our strength,
Fasting wears the weary soul,
Hajj's journey tests our resolve,
For truth's call can be perilous,
And lust, a tempest within our souls.

Money, oh so precious, eludes our grasp,
While chastity beckons, a noble struggle.
Honesty stands tall, harder than betrayal,
As we lower our gaze against desire's pull.

Remember my friend; our souls, ever inclined to desires,
in this life; the path to Paradise entwined with thorns,
Yet the road to Hell lies smooth and inviting.

Echo Verse 145 from surah An-Nisa

*4:145 Indeed, the hypocrites will be in
the lowest depths of the Fire - and never
will you find for them a helper -*

*Outright disbelief is more honorable than a
masked faith.
If hypocrisy weren't the gravest sin,
Allah would not cast the hypocrites
into the deepest pits of Fire.*

*In Mecca, the Arabs wore their beliefs with pride,
unblemished by the cowardice of deception.
But in Medina, a melting pot of races,
tensions rose, and politics thrived,
revealing the art of masks.*

*Here, as Islam grew strong,
those unwilling to embrace it
faced a choice:
to stand in their truth or to disguise their doubt.
In the end, resilience lies in authenticity;
our actions reveal our true beliefs,
for it is far heavier to carry the burden of hypocrisy
than to bear the weight of disbelief.*

Resilience Through Perseverance in Worship (Ibadah)

Theme: Staying consistent in worship during challenging times strengthens spiritual resilience.

Key Verse: *"And worship your Lord until there comes to you the certainty (death)."* (Surah Al-Hijr 15:99)

Echo Verse 12 from surah Maryam

19:12 [Allah] said, "O John, take the Scripture with determination." And We gave him judgement [while yet] a boy

---

It is not the strength of the hand but the resolve of the heart and the depth of its belief. So, take the book with strength, hold firm to your faith, and be unwavering in your conviction.

Even if the world is filled with wealth, stand firm. If all around you falter, do not waver in your righteousness.

This faith will triumph, with or without you, yet how noble it is to stand in its victory.

Why? Ask those who've tasted its sweetness;

Those who prayed two rak'ahs in the stillness of night, A feeling beyond words, a peace unmatched.

This faith is the wellspring of resilience, Lifting hearts, and fortifying souls.

Echo Verse 8 from surah Al Imran

3:8 [Who say], "Our Lord, let not our hearts deviate after You have guided us and grant us from Yourself mercy. Indeed, You are the Bestower.

What a profound supplication. To taste the sweetness of nearness to Allah is to fear the desolation of distance. So ask Allah to never deny you the joy of that closeness.

How many souls have drawn near, only to fall away? How many have sought Allah, then turned back? They believed that steadfastness was within their grasp, yet Allah, in His wisdom, turned them away from His door.

The obedient tremble more at the thought of losing their devotion than the disobedient fear their own rebellion.

Resilience in Speech (Qawlan Sadida)

Theme: Using measured, truthful speech in adversity promotes emotional and social resilience.

Key Verse: *"O you who have believed, fear Allah and speak words of appropriate justice."* (Surah Al-Ahzab 33:70)

Echo Verse 10 from surah Al-Qalam

68:10 And do not obey every worthless habitual swearer

Gossip is the force that divides communities and destroys relationships. And how abundant are the gossipers! When someone speaks well of another in their absence, you'll rarely find someone eager to carry that goodness back to them. But when ill is spoken behind someone's back, many rush to deliver the news.

The righteous of the past knew this well and would shut their doors to the bearers of gossip.

Al-Fadl ibn Ayyash narrated, "I was with Wahb ibn Munabbih when a man came and said, 'I passed by so-and-so, and he was cursing you.' Wahb responded, 'Could Satan not find a better messenger than you to bring me this news?'"

So do not become messengers of Satan, spreading what divides.

Echo Verse 18 from surah Qaf

50:18 Man does not utter any word except that with him is an observer prepared [to record]. He did not utter a word except that he had it.

Many angels are watching, not only recording the words that leave our mouths but also the words we post on social media.

A good word is written in the ledger of good deeds, and a bad word is inscribed in the record of bad deeds.

What you post will remain long after you've passed. If you cannot leave behind ongoing charity through your posts, at least ensure you do not leave behind an ongoing sin.

Keep your words clean and pure, so you do not regret them when the time comes for your account to be read.

Echo Verse 83 from surah Al-Baqarah

2:83 And [recall] when We took the covenant from the Children of Israel, [enjoining upon them], "Do not worship except Allah; and to parents do good and to relatives, orphans, and the needy. **And speak to people good [words]** *and establish prayer and give zakah." Then you turned away, except a few of you, and you were refusing.*

It is said that a kind word is a form of charity, a gentle whisper that opens doors, restores weary souls, and calms troubled minds.

Ishaq Ibn Rawiyya often encouraged his students to collect the Sahih Hadith. These words found their way into the heart of Al-Bukhari, who meticulously compiled the Sahih for our guidance.

"Your penmanship echoes that of the great scholars of Hadith," Al-Barzali once told his student Al-Dhahabi, instilling in him a profound love for the knowledge of Hadith.

Musab Al-Zubairi posed a question to Al-Shafi'i, asking, "Where do you stand in terms of jurisprudence?" This question, touched Al-Shafi'i's heart, who was fondness by poetry at that time, to shap him into the esteemed Imam we all revere today. Imam Ahmad declared, "Al-Shafi'i is like the sun, illuminating the world and bringing forth well-being and enlightenment to all."

Echo Verse 24 from surah Al-Fajr

89:24 He will say, "Oh, I wish I had sent ahead [some good] for my life."

In the echoes of the grave, the wishes of its inhabitants resonate: "Oh, how I wish I had done good for my life."

They realize that true life does not dwell on this earth; we are but travelers on our way to the everlasting.

The essence of our existence begins when we are laid in our graves; either as a garden of Paradise or a pit of Hell's depths.

If the people of the graves long for good deeds, then know that you are in the testing ground now.

This is your chance to choose rightly and pass the exam of life.

One day, Hasan al-Basri stood over a grave, observing a lifeless form, and he asked those gathered, "What do you think he wishes for now?" They replied, "If only he could return to do good deeds." Hasan replied, "You are now in the realm of his wishes, so strive and work while you still can."

Echo Verse 68 from surah Al-Anbiya

21:68 They said, "Burn him and support your gods - if you are to act."

The story of Abraham, peace be upon him, destroying the idols is a tale told countless times. Yet, hidden within it lies a linguistic treasure. The Qur'an doesn't just say his people wanted to burn him; the Arabic word means keep burning him to ashes. This subtle shift transforms the act from mere destruction to humiliation and hatred. They gathered wood for days, from the youngest to the eldest, casting Abraham into fire not just to kill him, but to disgrace him.

This isn't just about setting a flame; it's about stripping honor. The same is seen with Moses, peace be upon him, when he commanded the burning of the golden calf. Destroying it wasn't enough; it had to be reduced to ashes, scattered into nothingness.

This is the beauty of the Quran language; no two words are truly the same. Each carries its own weight, its own depth.

Resilience in Physical Health

Theme: Facing physical afflictions with patience and maintaining gratitude fosters resilience.

Key Verse: *"And when I am ill, it is He who cures me."* (Surah Ash-Shu'ara 26:80)

Echo Verse 31 from surah Al-Araf

7:31 O children of Adam, take your adornment at every masjid, and eat and drink, but be not excessive. Indeed, He likes not those who commit excess.

Physical health stands as a pillar of resilience in Islam, for a strong, well-tended body empowers a person to meet their duties and withstand the trials of life.

In Islam, the care of one's physical being is seen as an act of gratitude to Allah, a sacred trust in honor of the gift He has bestowed.

The Prophet taught us that the strong believer is better and dearer to our lord the weak believer, even there is good in both. not just in faith, but in body, mind, and spirit.

This resilience of the body is not isolated; it intertwines with spiritual and emotional strength, echoing the profound unity of well-being.

Through mindful nourishment, consistent exercise, and the wisdom of moderation, one fortifies the spirit, strengthens faith, and endures hardship with grace and resolve.

Resilience Through Remembrance (Dhikr)

Theme: Constantly remembering Allah during trials builds inner resilience and provides calm during hardship.

Key Verse: *"Those who have believed and whose hearts are assured by the remembrance of Allah. Unquestionably, by the remembrance of Allah hearts are assured."* (Surah Ar-Ra'd 13:28)

Echo Verse 143 from surah As-Saaffat

37:143 And had he not been of those who exalt Allah,

In times of joy, remember Allah; in moments of distress, call upon Him.

No one is more faithful than Allah, who has concealed within you hidden treasures of goodness.

So, when adversity strikes, let your heart turn to Him.

In prosperity, you can worship; in trials, you will find solace.

Remember, in every season of life, His presence is your greatest strength.

Echo Verse 152 from surah Al-Baqarah

2:152 So remember Me; I will remember you. And be grateful to Me and do not deny Me.

To be fair I don't know which brings me more joy;

the cause or the result, the reason or its outcome.

So, remember me, I remind you:

Allah, the Almighty, never disobeyed because of weakness; and is only obeyed as a generosity of Him to the mankind.

None can truly obey without receiving honor, for that is the beauty of obedience;

to know He has honored you. He has gazed upon your heart,

approved it, and inspired you to remember Him. What a promotion! What a grace!

So, rejoice in the result.

I remind you again: Reflect with your heart.

Let your tongue echo the remembrance, counting praises upon your fingers.

And know this;

The King of kings, the Sovereign of the heavens and the earth, remembers you.

If a worldly leader mentioned your name, your heart would soar with joy,

and sleep might escape you for the night.

But now, it is your Creator, the One who holds the dominion of all things, who remembers you.

Resilience in Facing Oppression and Tyranny

Theme: Enduring oppression and injustice with patience and faith, while trusting that Allah's justice will prevail. Example of that Maintaining faith and resilience under oppressive regimes or during political and social injustice

Key Verse: *"And do not think Allah is unaware of what the wrongdoers do. He only delays them for a Day when eyes will stare [in horror]."* (Surah Ibrahim 14:42)

Echo Verse 14 from surah Al-Qiyamah

75:14 Rather, man, against himself, will be a witness,

Praise for what you lack, brings no true gain, and criticism for faults not yours; often causes no pain.

No matter how virtuous you are, a hater will arise, even prophets faced disdain.

Goodness and virtue, though shining bright, Will always find shadows in the darkest night.

Immorality, too, finds its own embrace, Even Pharaoh and Nimrod had followers and love.

So, stand firm in righteous, let your heart be clear, for praise and blame are but echoes we hear.

Echo Verse 15 from surah Yusuf

12:15 So when they took him [out] and agreed to put him into the bottom of the well... But We inspired to him, "You will surely inform them [someday] about this affair of theirs while they do not perceive [your identity]."

The boy, cast into the depths of a pit,
Rescued by a bucket, his worth dismissed as mere grit,
Yet from such humble beginnings, a destiny unfolds;
He is destined to rise, to become Egypt's Minister.

Remember, a hard chapter may merely set the stage,
A prelude to beauty that blossoms with age.
In the tapestry of life, trust in Allah's embrace,
For every dark moment can lead to a brighter place.

Echo Verse 26 from surah Nuh

71:26 And Noah said, "My Lord, do not leave upon the earth from among the disbelievers an inhabitant.

The first weapon of mass destruction wielded on earth; was not made of steel or stone, but rose when
Noah, peace be upon him,
Lifted his hands to the heavens alone.
He pleaded, "My Lord, leave not a trace
Of the disbelievers' dwelling place."
Beware those who reject the signs,
For refuge lies in Allah's care,
And supplication becomes their weapon,
Sharper than any sword laid bare.

Resilience Through Charity (Zakat and Sadaqah)

Theme: Even when faced with economic difficulties, giving charity strengthens social and personal resilience by fostering empathy and solidarity.

Key Verse: *"The example of those who spend their wealth in the way of Allah is like a seed [of grain] that sprouts seven ears; in every ear is a hundred grains..."* (Surah Al-Baqarah 2:261)

Echo Verse 245 from surah Al-Baqarah

"Who is it that would loan Allah a goodly loan so He may multiply it for him many times over?"

This verse always leaves me in awe, reflecting on the immense generosity of Allah. He invites us to do good, promising to multiply our deeds, though no act of ours could ever harm or benefit the Almighty.

He asks us to be kind, not for His sake, but for ours; so we may flourish in goodness.

Who can give to Allah, the Most Generous, a loan of faith and kindness, only to see it returned beyond measure, showered with blessings? Give with a sincere heart, and receive more than you can imagine. What a faith, where Allah rewards us for what is truly His.

What a blessing it is to be a Muslim. A smile earns reward, a sneeze brings mercy. A simple greeting of peace earns reward, and when illness strikes, sins are wiped away. And when they are gone, we are elevated in rank. The Lord, in His generosity, multiplies our good deeds.

Even when we sin, forgiveness is near.

Truly, what a faith; filled with mercy, blessings, and endless grace.

Echo Verse 22 from surah An-Nur

24:22 And let not those of virtue among you and wealth swear not to give [aid] to their relatives and the needy and the emigrants for the cause of Allah, and let them pardon and overlook. Would you not like that Allah should forgive you? And Allah is Forgiving and Merciful.

One day, the Prophet, may Allah bless him and grant him peace, called upon the people to give charity. Alabah ibn Zaid, poor and without means, could not find anything material to offer.

So, he stood and said, "O Messenger of Allah, I have nothing to give, but I offer my honor for the sake of Allah. I forgive anyone who has wronged me."

The next day, the Prophet, peace and blessings be upon him, asked, "Where is Ibn Zaid's companion?" Alabah stood and replied, "Here I am, O Messenger of Allah." The Prophet then said, "Allah has accepted your charity."

Charity is not only about money; Allah Almighty loves most the servant adorned with good manners, and among the most beloved qualities to Him is forgiveness. His love for those who pardon and forgive others surpasses all.

Resilience in Building Societal Bonds

Theme: Strengthening societal ties and working together to face communal challenges fosters collective resilience.

Key Verse: *"And hold firmly to the rope of Allah all together and do not become divided."* (Surah Al-Imran 3:103)

Echo Verse 23 from surah Al-Furqan

25:23 And We will regard what they have done of deeds and make them as dust dispersed.

Indeed, our Lord neither overlooks nor forgets. Beware, for your deeds are not lost; they follow you.

You have misled others, and your intentions may stray if you worship Allah for the sake of others, risking the loss of your good deeds tomorrow.

Reflect on the hearts you have broken, the wealth you have unjustly taken, the honor you have tarnished, and the jobs you have stolen through deceit.

Justice awaits, so purify your actions before it's too late.

Echo Verse 4 from surah At-Tin

95:4 We have certainly created man in the best of stature;

True beauty is not defined by handsomeness or fair hair; it lies within the miracle of creation; the body that serves as a vessel of purpose. Just as Allah distributes wealth and sustenance among His creation, so too is beauty a divine allocation.

Consider Luqman the Wise, a slave from Nubia, and Bilal bin Rabah, whose dark skin bore no harm to their dignity. For in the eyes of Allah, handsomeness is of little consequence to the hearts of the unfaithful, which are destined to be consumed by fire.

Do not mock another's appearance; remember, you did not create yourself. If you cannot respect the creation, at least be courteous to the Creator. Your laughter should not lead another to pain, for sometimes a hurtful tongue cuts deeper than the sharpest sword. Choose your words wisely, for they hold the power to heal or to harm.

Echo Verse 21 from surah Yusuf

12:21 And the one from Egypt who bought him said to his wife, "Make his residence comfortable. Perhaps he will benefit us, or we will adopt him as a son." And thus, We established Joseph in the land that We might teach him the interpretation of events. And Allah is predominant over His affair, but most of the people do not know.

Can you see it?

Once more reflection on the story of Joseph; the one who is his blood and stands near;

He commanded, 'Let him perish.' Yet for the stranger, he decreed, 'Honor him.'

Love, a divine sustenance from God,

You may never know in which heart this gift has been bestowed.

Echo Verse 97 from surah Al-Hijr

15:97 And We already know that your chest is constrained by what they say.

A harsh word stings like a sword,
While a sweet word brings joy, a treasured reward.
Revelation came, and Gabriel drew near,
Taking him from Mecca to Jerusalem, clear,
To lead the prophets in prayer, a role divine,
Embracing the leadership of mankind, a sacred sign.

He ascended to heavens, where no prophet has tread,
Where Allah bestowed Al-Kawthar, blessings widespread.
Yet harsh words pierced him, causing pain to his chest,
Taste your words before they take flight,
If sweet on your tongue, they'll bring joy and light.
But if bitter, they'll echo with sorrow and pain,
be in control.

Beautiful goals cannot rise from methods so crude,
Align your approach to the aims you pursue.
For the Prophet's call rings true and clear,
And gentle whispers remind us to steer.

Echo Verse 19 from surah An-Nisa

4:19 O you who have believed, it is not lawful for you to inherit women by compulsion. And do not make difficulties for them in order to take [back] part of what you gave them unless they commit a clear immorality. **And live with them in kindness.** *For if you dislike them - perhaps you dislike a thing and Allah makes therein much good.*

Kindness is a tapestry, woven wide,
Embracing all, a gentle guide.
A smile gracing her face, a sweet word's grace,
Hugs shared close, love's warm embrace.

Listening to her complaints, nurturing her health,
Respecting her voice, honoring her wealth.
Supporting her passions, her faith, and her dreams,
Helping with children, like soft, flowing streams.

In moments of pain, a tender hand to lend,
Tolerating moods, true strength to defend.
Seek truth in expressions, let wisdom unfold,
For kindness is strength, a treasure to hold.

The Prophet, blessed be his name,
A master of kindness
With family, he served, a smile on his face,
His final command: treat your females with kindness.

Resilience in Ethical Conduct (Husn al-Khulq)

Theme: Upholding ethical principles despite societal pressure fosters internal resilience.

Key Verse: *"Indeed, Allah orders justice and good conduct and giving to relatives and forbids immorality, bad conduct, and oppression."* (Surah An-Nahl 16:90)

Echo Verse 18 from surah Luqman

31:18 And do not turn your cheek [in contempt] toward people and do not walk through the earth exultantly. Indeed, Allah does not like everyone self-deluded and boastful.

As passed down through generations, Yahya ibn Ma'in once said: "I have never seen anyone like Ahmad ibn Hanbal. He was among us for 50 years, yet he never boasted of his righteousness or goodness." Ahmad would often say, "We are a poor people.

Money, when it makes you arrogant, is true poverty.

Knowledge, when it makes you proud, is ignorance.

Position, when it makes you tyrannical, is a downfall.

And power, when it makes you haughty, is but weakness.

True wealth, honor, and wisdom are found in those who remain humble.

Echo Verse 229 from surah Al-Baqarah

2:229 Divorce is twice. Then, either keep [her] in an acceptable manner or release [her] with good treatment.

Cherish her with kindness, or

Let her go with grace.

Do not mourn the end of relationships;

For life, too, will one day cease.

What saddens me is not the farewell,

But the manner in which it concludes.

I prefer to part with a warm embrace,

Like bidding a dear one farewell at the gate,

Not leaving with wounds as if from battle,

But with a heart full of gratitude,

For every moment shared.

Echo Verse 85 from surah Al-Maidah

5:85 So **Allah rewarded them for what they said** with gardens [in Paradise] beneath which rivers flow, wherein they abide eternally. And that is the reward of doers of good.

Verse 64 from surah Al-Maidah

5:64 And the Jews say, "The hand of Allah is chained." Chained are their hands, **and cursed are they for what they say.** Rather, both His hands are extended; He spends however He wills.

One word can lead you to Paradise, and another can cast you into Hell. The Prophet, peace and blessings be upon him, once said to Muadh, while pointing to his own tongue, "Guard this."

Muadh, puzzled, asked, "Will we truly be held accountable for what we say, O Messenger of Allah?"

The Prophet elaborated, "Is there anything that drags people face-first into Hellfire more than the careless utterances of their tongues?"

Beware, for the tongue wields a power unseen; a word spoken lightly may weigh heavily in the Hereafter.

I look around now, and see people swearing in every sentence; remember, every word is written.

Do you wish your record to be filled with curses, or with words of remembrance for your Lord?

Echo Verse 3 from surah At-Tahreem

66:3 And [remember] when the Prophet confided to one of his wives a statement; and when she informed [another] of it and Allah showed it to him, he made known part of it and ignored a part. And when he informed her about it, she said, "Who told you this?" He said, "I was informed by the Knowing, the Acquainted."

Sometimes, silence speaks volumes, for certain problems only grow deeper through words. The Prophet Muhammad (peace be upon him) taught us, "Whoever believes in Allah and the Last Day should either speak a good word or remain silent" (Sahih al-Bukhari). This profound wisdom reminds us of the power of our words and the importance of choosing silence over harmful or unnecessary chatter.

Consider the story of Luqman al-Hakim, known as Luqman the Wise, who imparted this valuable lesson to his son: "O my son, if you have nothing good to say, then be silent." His wisdom highlights how unnecessary discourse can lead to misunderstanding and conflict. In the quiet moments, we often find clarity and peace, while in the noise of thoughtless words, we may only sow discord.

Resilience Through Gratitude (Shukr)

Theme: Gratitude as a way of fostering resilience by focusing on what one has, rather than what one lacks. Even during tough times, maintaining gratitude is a powerful way to cultivate resilience.

Key Verse: "And [remember] when your Lord proclaimed, 'If you are grateful, I will surely increase you [in favor]; but if you deny, indeed, My punishment is severe.'" (Surah Ibrahim 14:7)

Echo Verse 23 from surah Al-Mulk

67:23 Say, "It is He who has produced you and made for you hearing and vision and hearts; little are you grateful."

There was once a righteous man; bald of head, frail in body, blind in sight, and paralyzed in limbs; yet he would say, "Praise be to Allah, who has spared me from what has afflicted many of His creation." A passerby, astonished, asked him, "Blind, leprous, bald, and paralyzed; what has He spared you from?"

The man replied, "Woe to you! He has blessed me with a tongue that remembers Him, a heart that is thankful, and a body that endures affliction with patience.

People often believe that wealth is the only blessing worthy of gratitude, yet they forget the gift of sight while others are blind, the hands that give and receive while others are immobile, and the legs that walk while others are confined. O Lord, praise be to You for even the simplest of movements, for every breath and step is a mercy untold.

Echo Verse 98 from surah Al-Kahf

18:98 [Dhul-Qarnayn] said, "This is a mercy from my Lord; but when the promise of my Lord comes, He will make it level, and ever is the promise of my Lord true."

*Dhul-Qarnayn, with iron turned to flame,
Poured molten metal and raised a wall, a mighty frame,
To seal in Yajuj and Majuj, imprisoned tight,
And spoke, "This is my Lord's mercy, a testament of His might."*

*Solomon, in but a blink of eye,
Brought Bilqis' throne from far-off Yemen's sky,
And said, "From my Lord, this grace is drawn."
For all returns to Allah, the Almighty, the One.*

Be grateful

Echo Verse 34 from surah Ibrahim

14:34 And He gave you from all you asked of Him. And if you should count the favor of Allah, you could not enumerate them. Indeed, mankind is [generally] most unjust and ungrateful.

Who asked of Him and was left unheard?
He is Allah, the Fulfiller of every word.
Whoever came to Him trembling in fear,
But did not find His protection near?

Who begged at His door, hands open wide,
But was not given the help He provides?

Seek Him, dear soul, at the proper hour,
In the last third of night, feel His power.
Stand before Him, and ask without fear,
For He draws the sincere ever near.

Trust in your Lord, be patient and sure,
Empty hands lifted will always endure.
They will return to you, full and complete,
For His mercy is vast, His love is sweet.

Before all this, let your food be pure,
From sources that are good and secure.
As our Prophet explained, make what you consume,
Good and halal, and prayers will bloom.

So, trust in His promise, trust in His way,
Your Lord will answer whatever you pray.

Echo Verse 66 from surah Hud

11:66 So when Our command came, We saved Salih and those who believed with him, by mercy from Us, and [saved them] from the disgrace of that day. Indeed, it is your Lord who is the Powerful, the Exalted in Might.

Reflect deeply and recognize it well; it is by mercy from Allah. When relief arrives after distress, know that it is by His mercy, not by your own efforts. If healing follows illness, do not attribute it solely to medicine or the doctor, but to the mercy of Allah. When a job comes after a long period of unemployment, it is not merely your qualifications or abilities at work, but the mercy of your Lord that opens the door.

And if a child is granted after years of longing and despair, it is not your strength or the remedy that brings life, but the mercy of Allah. These are but causes, and none of them can harm or benefit until He permits.

How many are treated yet remain unhealed? How many hold degrees yet stay jobless? How many are married but childless? All goodness comes to you by Allah's mercy, not by mere means. So, acknowledge the true Giver, and give credit where it is due, to the One who bestows without measure.

Echo Verse 23 from surah Al-Mulk

67:23 Say, "It is He who has produced you and made for you hearing and vision and hearts; little are you grateful."

Little do we give thanks. Allah has bestowed upon us blessings until they seemed our right, and in our hearts, we withheld our gratitude. We buy what we desire, forgetting the One who provided the wealth. We come and go with vigor, yet forget the Giver of health. We pass by hospitals, unaware of the well-being we've been granted. We walk by prisons, oblivious to the freedom bestowed upon us. We watch death and ruin on screens, yet overlook the One who has gifted us security.

The gravest illness of the heart is becoming accustomed to the blessings and gifts from our Lord, taking them for granted until they slip from our grasp. Only then do we realize their true value, but by then, they may be lost to us. True wisdom lies in appreciating Allah's favors while they are still with us.

The house that shields you is a blessing; look upon the homeless. The spouse who holds you close is a blessing; see the sorrow of the widows. The child who runs to you with joy is a blessing; consider those denied the gift of children.

We are surrounded by the infinite blessings of Allah, yet we often struggle to show our gratitude; a simple pause, a quiet word of thanks. So, let us say with steadfast hearts:

"O Allah, all praise belongs to You. Praise that is beyond measure, equal to the countless praises of Your creation, from the moment this word of praise existed until its end. And I believe it will never end, for true praise is eternal."

Resilience in Facing Temptations

Theme: The Quran encourages believers to resist temptations that can weaken their resolve and spiritual resilience.

Key Verse: "And those who strive for Us – We will surely guide them to Our ways. And indeed, Allah is with the doers of good." (Surah Al-Ankabut 29:69)

Echo Verse 20 from surah Al-Hadid

57:20 Know that the life of this world is but amusement and diversion and adornment and boasting to one another and competition in increase of wealth and children - like the example of a rain whose [resulting] plant growth pleases the tillers; then it dries and you see it turned yellow; then it becomes [scattered] debris. And in the Hereafter is severe punishment and forgiveness from Allah and approval. And what is the worldly life except the enjoyment of delusion.

The world is but a fleeting enjoyment, a reality grasped by those who truly see. It offers no true friendship, ultimately abandoning all who cling to it. The wise person understands: it is best to use it to collect good deeds.

When Omar bin Al-Khattab visited the Levant, he turned to Abu Ubaidah and said, "Show us your home." Upon entering, Omar observed, "Where are your possessions? I see nothing here."

Abu Ubaidah simply said, "What you see is all I have." Omar asked, "Do you have any food?" Abu Ubaidah then rose, retrieving a bowl of bread. Seeing this, Omar shed tears and exclaimed, "We are all obsessed with this world, except you, O Abu Ubaidah!"

In that moment, Abu Ubaidah held the title of prince over the Muslims in the Levant, yet his heart remained unburdened by worldly desires.

Echo Verse 12 from surah Al-Mulk

67:12 Indeed, those who fear their Lord unseen will have forgiveness and great reward.

They were hidden from the gaze of people, yet they knew; always; that Allah's eye was upon them. So, they turned away from the forbidden, though their hands could have grasped it. They suppressed their desires, standing firm against the pull of temptation. They forsook sin, though it was easy and within reach.

But they did not shun lust out of disdain, nor did they refuse forbidden wealth from a hatred of gold. No, they abandoned it all for the sake of Allah alone. They felt the weight of His watchful presence and were humbled.

This is the essence of fearing the King of Kings, leaving behind indulgence not out of fear of scandal, but out of awe for the One who sees all.

Resilience Through Silence and Thoughtful Reflection

Theme: Resilience is also linked to thoughtful reflection and the ability to maintain silence in challenging situations.

Key Verse: *"Do not pursue that of which you have no knowledge. Indeed, the hearing, the sight, and the heart – about all those [one] will be questioned."* (Surah Al-Isra 17:36)

Echo Verse 4 from surah Yusuf

12:4 [Of these stories mention] when Joseph said to his father, "O my father, indeed I have seen [in a dream] eleven stars and the sun and the moon; I saw them prostrating to me."

Know well where you keep your secrets. Not every person is worthy of your trust, and not every matter is fit to be shared.

Guard your inner world carefully, for not all should be revealed. In your dealings with others, keep a part of yourself reserved; leave something of yourself just for you.

especially in matters between you and your Lord.

Do good deeds in secret, without seeking the eyes of others. Don't show off, for those hidden acts may be your salvation on the Day of Judgment. What remains unseen in this world could be the very thing that brings light to your account in the Hereafter.

Echo Verse 77 from surah Al-Kahf

18:77 So they set out, until when they came to the people of a town, they asked its people for food, but they refused to offer them hospitality. And they found therein a wall about to collapse, so al-Khidh r restored it. [Moses] said, "If you wished, you could have taken for it a payment."

When they fail to see your worth, recall the tale of Moses and Al-Khidr, peace be upon them. They wandered the earth, seeking hospitality, yet found no open door, no morsel of bread to share.

Though they were among the most righteous souls of their time, they faced mistreatment and scorn. Let this remind you to know your own value.

In moments of doubt, sit in stillness; lay your head upon your pillow, and let your mind find peace, even as others cast their harsh accusations. For a clear conscience is a treasure beyond measure, a light that guides you through the darkest hours.

Echo Verse 16 from surah Al-Kahf

18:16 [The youths said to one another], "And when you have withdrawn from them and that which they worship other than Allah, retreat to the cave. Your Lord will spread out for you of His mercy and will prepare for you from your affair facility."

How strange is this faith; when hearts of people turn to stone,
Yet God softens mountains with mercy alone for these young people.

like the prophet; they end up in a cave, seeking refuge and light,
For when faith is a crime, the rock becomes life.

Wherever one's faith finds a place to belong,
Their roots run deep, even when they feel wronged.
What the Prophet left behind in Mecca's embrace,
Was love for the land, yet marked by disgrace.

With tears in his eyes, he bid farewell,
"By God, you're beloved, but I must rebel.
Had it not been for those who forced me away,
I would have remained; I would have chosen to stay."

Kingship and riches were offered with might,
Yet he turned from temptation, embracing the light.
"Leave this to God; let His will unfold,
For the truth of my heart cannot be bought or sold."

Resilience Through Being Dutiful to Parents (Birr al-Walidayn)

Theme: Families play an important role in providing emotional strength and resilience in facing challenges.

Key Verse: "And We have enjoined upon man [care] for his parents. His mother carried him, [increasing her] in weakness upon weakness, and his weaning is in two years." (Surah Luqman 31:14)

Echo Verse 8 from surah Al-Ankabut

29:8 And We have enjoined upon man goodness to parents. But if they endeavor to make you associate with Me that of which you have no knowledge, do not obey them. To Me is your return, and I will inform you about what you used to do.

How quickly we forget:

Our parents, the reason we breathe in this life.

Do you grasp the odds that make you, uniquely you?

Countless, beyond measure.

They nurtured you in youth, prayed for your growth,

Yet when they grow old and frail,

Do we not often wish their passing would be swift,

For our own relief, weary from their care?

But they are the true essence of resilience.

To care for them is to repay, in part,

The boundless love they poured into you.

Families are our roots, grounding us deep,

As life's storms test our strength and resolve.

In parents' quiet sacrifices, we find the well of endurance,

The unspoken resilience that shapes who we are.

In honoring them, we strengthen our souls,

Pleasing our Lord, gaining blessings in this life and the next.

Resilience in Brotherhood and Sisterhood (Ukhuwah)

Theme: Building strong brotherhood and sisterhood in faith helps in resilience through communal support.

Key Verse: *"The believers are but brothers, so make settlement between your brothers. And fear Allah that you may receive mercy."* (Surah Al-Hujurat 49:10)

Echo Verse 11 from surah Al-Mujadilah

58:11 O you who have believed, when you are told, "Space yourselves" in assemblies, then make space; Allah will make space for you. And when you are told, "Arise," then arise; Allah will raise those who have believed among you and those who were given knowledge, by degrees. And Allah is Acquainted with what you do.

The verse was revealed regarding making space in gatherings, but its meaning extends far beyond that. It speaks of generosity in all forms.

Whoever shows generosity to those who resist or are hardened by him, Allah will expand upon him in return.

Whoever brings peace to troubled thoughts, Allah will soothe his own.

Whoever brings joy to a heart, Allah will fill his heart with joy.

Whoever eases another's pain, Allah will ease his pain.

Whoever wipes away a tear, Allah will wipe away his tears.

There is none more generous, none more faithful, than Allah Almighty. And truly, good deeds shield us from evil.

Echo Verse 18 from surah Al-Kahf

18:18 And you would think them awake, while they were asleep. And We turned them to the right and to the left, while their dog stretched his forelegs at the entrance. If you had looked at them, you would have turned from them in flight and been filled by them with terror.

In the Qur'an, a dog is immortalized for its good company,

So, choose your friends as carefully as you choose your clothes,

For the companion you cherish can shape your soul.

Seek to uplift others, but beware;

For they may pull you down instead.

Often, we adopt the faith of those we hold dear.

Wise people choose companions before they travel,

And neighbors before they build their homes.

A true friend is life's treasure,

A well where secrets dwell,

A shoulder to lean on, a hand to lighten your load.

What troubles you? Remember the dog,

Honored for its loyalty in noble company,

And the whale that bears the burden of Yunus, peace be upon him.

Even the ant thrives through Solomon's smile,

And we, too, deserve such remembrance;

For in friendship, we find both burdens and joys.

Echo Verse 21 from surah Ar-Rum

30:21 And of His signs is that He created for you from yourselves mates that you may find tranquility in them; and He placed between you affection and mercy. Indeed, in that are signs for a people who give thought.

God created Eve from Adam's rib, not from the dust, to show that she is part of him, and he feels that connection deeply.

This divine wisdom ensures that man and woman are drawn to each other, not just to share a home, but to complete one another.

Just as man protects his eyes, he guards his wife, for without her, his life is incomplete. And woman, in turn, longs for him, as one yearns for home.

Together, they are not just two; they are one, bound by love, designed to sustain life and harmony on earth.

Resilience Through Repentance (Tawbah)

Theme: Resilience in the face of past mistakes through constantly seeking Allah's forgiveness and moving forward.

Key Verse: *"Indeed, Allah loves those who are constantly repentant and loves those who purify themselves."* (Surah Al-Baqarah 2:222)

Echo Verse 133 from surah Al Imran

3:133 And hasten to forgiveness from your Lord and a garden as wide as the heavens and earth, prepared for the righteous

---

Ibn al-Qayyim, may Allah have mercy on him, would often say: The best day for any servant is the day of his sincere repentance to Allah.

When someone holds a loved one dear and a conflict arises between them, they will do everything to reconcile, finding creative ways to mend the relationship. And who is more deserving of appeasement than Allah, the Most High?

So, if you commit an act that disrupts your love for your Lord, rush to repentance; sometimes through charity, sometimes through seeking forgiveness, prayer, or reciting the Quran.

Hurry, for death does not wait for the dawn,

I say, "Tomorrow I'll change," but tomorrow is gone.

The length of our hopes, so endless, so vain,

Believing that death is far from our lane.

But those who've passed, just moments ago,

Thought the same, unaware of the final blow.

So hurry, don't wait, for time slips away,

An hour's delay may close Heaven's gate today.

Seize this moment, before it is lost,

For the price of delay is too high a cost.

Paradise awaits, but only for those

Who hurry now, before life's final close.

Echo Verse 50 from surah Al-Kahf

18:50 And [mention] when We said to the angels, "Prostrate to Adam," and they prostrated, except for Iblees. He was of the jinn and departed from the command of his Lord. Then will you take him and his descendants as allies other than Me while they are enemies to you? Wretched it is for the wrongdoers as an exchange.

Iblees' refusal to prostrate, as Allah had commanded him, became the reason for his expulsion from Allah's mercy.

But if we pause and reflect on the state of Iblees and compare it to the condition of Muslims who abandon prayer, a striking similarity appears.

We marvel at how Satan refused to bow to Adam, yet those who neglect prayer refuse to bow to the Lord of Adam. SubhanAllah! How merciful and generous Allah is to this nation.

He calls His servants back to Him, morning and evening, no matter how great the crime, how heavy the sin, or how long they have turned away.

Echo Verse 32 from surah Qaf

50:32 [It will be said], "This is what you were promised - for every returner [to Allah] and keeper [of His covenant]

The verse is profound, for Allah, the Mighty, speaks of those who sin yet continually return to Him. The Merciful understands our weaknesses; His door remains ever open for those who seek Him. He even promises Paradise to those who persist in repentance.

But beware of allowing your sins to fill you with arrogance in the face of Allah's mercy, yet do not belittle them when confronted with His punishment. Strive to remain balanced, walking the line between hope and fear; hope in His boundless mercy, and fear of His just retribution.

Do not let Satan shame you for your transgressions; return to your Lord, for He calls Himself the Forgiving precisely because we sin and He invites us to repent. So, if you find yourself faltering a thousand times in a single day, return to Allah with a thousand sincere repentances.

Echo Verse 165 from surah Al Imran

3:165 Why [is it that] when a [single] disaster struck you [on the day of Uhud], although you had struck [the enemy in the battle of Badr] with one twice as great, you said, "From where is this?" Say, "It is from yourselves." Indeed, Allah is over all things competent.

"Say, 'It is from within yourselves.' If troubles or defeat weigh upon you, look inward. Allah, the Almighty, tests you not to burden, but to mend what only trial can heal.

History whispers to us of the time when the skies withheld their rain in the days of Solomon, peace be upon him.

He led his people out to pray for rain, but before them, he saw an ant, its tiny hands raised to the heavens, pleading, 'O Allah, affliction falls upon us only through sin, and it is lifted by repentance alone. We are but part of Your creation, servants among Your servants. Do not let the sins of Adam's children ruin us.'

Then, Solomon, peace be upon him, turned to his people and said, 'Return home, for the prayer of this ant has been heard.'"

Echo Verse 222 from surah Al-Baqarah

2:222 Indeed, Allah loves those who are constantly repentant and loves those who purify themselves."

It speaks to the profound nature of repentance, a constant return to the Divine. For one to repent often suggests a life of many mistakes, yet in this lies the beauty of God's mercy. Notice the perfection in His words. Glory be to Him; He did not simply say He forgives or pardons those who repent. No, He declared that He loves those who repent.

Yes, He loves those who sin and then return, who disobey by day but seek Him by night. Allah Almighty did not convey His love for those who repent because we sin. Rather, He refuses to let Satan stand between us and Him. He is telling us, no matter how great the sin, His mercy is greater. No matter how frequent our failings, Allah does not tire of pardoning us; until we tire of returning to Him.

Keep something of yourself for yourself, detached from the world. Do not be deceived by the fleeting pleasures of this life, and do not let illusions lead you astray from Allah's boundless mercy.

Resilience Through Balancing Worldly Life and the Hereafter

Theme: Achieving resilience by balancing one's focus on the worldly life and the afterlife without becoming overly attached to either. Maintaining hope in eternal rewards during worldly suffering builds resilience by shifting focus from temporary difficulties to lasting rewards.

Key Verse: *"But seek, through that which Allah has given you, the home of the Hereafter; and [yet], do not forget your share of the world."* (Surah Al-Qasas 28:77)

Echo Verse 5 from surah Fatir

35:5 O mankind, indeed the promise of Allah is truth, so let not the worldly life delude you and be not deceived about Allah by the Deceiver.

Do not be deceived by the fleeting mirage of this world. Its life, no matter how vast it seems, is but a passing breath. Even to Noah; peace be upon him; who lived beyond a thousand years, it was short. When asked why he built a house of reeds, he replied, "This is the home of the transient." Time, though it stretches, shrinks in the grasp of those who endure it. The Prophet, may Allah bless him and grant him peace, teaches us to have no real bond with this world and be like a traveler who sought shade beneath a tree, then moved on, leaving it behind.

Even if the world grows immense in your eyes, its worth is less than a mosquito's wing to Allah. Whatever the disbeliever drinks from it is but a sip, soon gone. If you believe it will last, remember the words of Caliph Al-Mansour to the spring: "How sweet life would be, if not for death." Al-Rabi answered him, "Life is only sweet because of death." When Al-Mansour asked him how, he said, "Without death, the kingdom would not have reached you."

Echo Verse 185 from surah Al Imran

3:185 Every soul will taste death, and you will only be given your [full] compensation on the Day of Resurrection. So, he who is drawn away from the Fire and admitted to Paradise has attained [his desire]. And what is the life of this world except the enjoyment of delusion.

Death is the cup from which all will drink; the believer and the immoral, the prophet, the tyrant, the jinn and the angels, and none other than Allah remains.

Death is not the end of the story, on the contrary, it is only the beginning. The problem is, we will only truly realize this when it is too late.

Echo Verse 22 from surah Al-Qiyamah

75:22 [Some] faces, that Day, will be radiant, looking at him.

The most beautiful bliss of Paradise is not in its beautiful trees, a beautiful thing indeed. It is not about its rivers, even though we all know it would be a breathtaking view.

The most beautiful thing we are all seeking is seeing the face of our Lord Almighty. So, if the people of Paradise enter Paradise, Allah asks, "Do you want something more for you?" They say, "Did you not enter us into Paradise, whiten our faces, and save us from the Fire?"

Then he removes the veil from his honorable face. That is when they realize that they were not given anything dearer to them than looking at their Lord, the Almighty.

Echo Verse 4 from surah Az-Zalzalah

99:4 That Day, it will report its news

Every place where you bowed in worship will stand as your witness. And every place where you disobeyed will testify against you. So, multiply your righteous witnesses. In every spot you tread, leave behind a prostration. In every city you visit, give charity. In every village, seek refuge in the mosque.

This earth beneath your feet is not just dust and gravel. It is the silent observer of your deeds, the chief witness in the most just court; the court of Allah Almighty. His judgment encompasses all of creation, and nothing escapes his reach.

Echo Verse 55 from surah Ta-Ha

20:55 From the earth We created you, and into it We will return you, and from it We will extract you another time.

A life rich with knowledge,

With a loving wife and children, with wealth;

But then, what lies beyond the door?

Under the soil they put us,

Embarking on a journey to our final fate,

Life is but a passage, a fleeting quest,

Ask Noah, he lived 1000 years, maybe more, where is he now?

Choose your path carefully,

For each step you take here,

It will define your outcome; Heaven's embrace or the fire's weight

---

Echo Verse 16 from surah Luqman

31:16 [And Luqman said], "O my son, indeed if wrong should be the weight of a mustard seed and should be within a rock or [anywhere] in the heavens or in the earth, Allah will bring it forth. Indeed, Allah is Subtle and Acquainted.

You asked of Allah, seeking no help from men,

For every wish you entrusted to Him,

For every supplication, whispered then forgotten;

Yet Allah, the All-Knowing, never forgets.

For every longing that stirred tears in your eyes,

For all you desired with a heart so full;

Be certain, Allah will bring it to pass.

Indeed, He is gentle, wise beyond measure,

The Most Generous, with both hands giving.

Trust in His mercy, for He is the All-Kind,

And His knowledge encompasses all things.

Epilogue

At this stage, we have journeyed through the Quran and uncovered numerous themes that refine our understanding of resilience. Yet, all this knowledge is incomplete without the cornerstone that holds it all together. I have saved the best for last.

Tawheed; the belief in the oneness of Allah; is the core and foundation of Islamic faith and the ultimate pillar of resilience from a Divine perspective. Without a firm belief in **Tawheed**, the entire structure of Islamic thought, including resilience, lacks its grounding. Believing in the oneness of Allah provides the spiritual foundation upon which all other acts, values, and behaviors are built.

> ***Key Verse:*** *"Say, 'He is Allah, [who is] One, Allah, the Eternal Refuge. He neither begets nor is born, nor is there to Him any equivalent.'" (Surah Al-Ikhlas 112:1-4)*

This verse, Surah Al-Ikhlas, is one of the most concise yet profound summaries of **Tawheed**, asserting Allah's singularity, which is the bedrock of Islamic faith and resilience.

Why Tawheed is the Core Pillar of Resilience:

- ❖ **Ultimate Trust and Reliance on Allah**: Tawheed teaches that Allah is the sole creator, sustainer, and controller of everything in existence. This belief gives a person the strength to endure hardships, knowing that everything that happens is by the will of Allah and is part of His divine wisdom.

- ❖ **Resilience through Surrender**: True resilience in Islam is rooted in surrendering to the will of Allah (Islam means submission). Belief in Tawheed helps a person accept trials with patience, knowing that their outcome is in the hands of the One who knows all.
- ❖ **Purpose and Meaning in Hardships**: Tawheed gives purpose to life's struggles because it frames challenges as tests from Allah, which, if faced with faith, lead to spiritual growth and ultimately to reward in the Hereafter.
- ❖ **Liberation from Fear**: A believer grounded in Tawheed is not swayed by fear of loss, societal pressures, or adversity, because they place their ultimate hope and fear in Allah alone, not in worldly matters. This fosters immense internal strength.

Here we have it, we have discovered 45 resilience elements from Quran. Now it is time to develop a comprehensive resilience theory, let's apply systems thinking by recognizing the interconnectedness of these themes. Systems thinking, at its core, emphasizes understanding how individual parts influence one another within a whole. Here, resilience is not just a personal trait but a dynamic process supported by spiritual, emotional, and social structures found in Islamic teachings.

Core Categories of Resilience

From the provided elements, we can organize the resilience framework into nine major interconnected core categories:

1. Spiritual Core

Definition: This category emphasizes the internal strength drawn from faith, belief in divine purpose, and submission to Allah's will. Spiritual resilience provides the core energy needed to remain steadfast during trials.

- **Key Elements**:
    - **Tawheed** (Oneness of Allah)
    - **Niyyah** (Intention)
    - **Tasleem** (Submission to Allah)
    - **Tawakkul** (Reliance on Allah)
    - **Qadr** (Divine Decree)
    - **Dhikr** (Remembrance of Allah)
    - **Sabr** (Patience)
    - **Ibadah** (Perseverance in Worship)
    - **Dawah** (Patience in Spreading Faith)
    - **Tazkiyah** (Spiritual Purification)
    - **Tawbah** (Repentance)
    - **Balance** (Worldly Life and Hereafter)

System Role: The Spiritual Core serves as the input system; the internal beliefs, intentions, and purpose that shape resilience. This core integrates with emotional and social dimensions, providing inner stability that sustains the individual throughout life's trials.

2. Cognitive Core

Definition: Cognitive resilience is built through knowledge acquisition and mental clarity. It involves using intellect and wisdom to solve problems and navigate life's complexities.

- **Key Elements**:
    - **Ilm** (Knowledge)
    - **Reflection and Thoughtful Speech (Qawlan Sadida)**
    - **Critical Thinking** for navigating adversity

System Role: The Cognitive Core is the decision-making system that processes challenges, applies wisdom, and provides insight for adaptive strategies. It ensures actions are purposeful and aligned with spiritual intentions.

3. Emotional Core

Definition: This category focuses on regulating emotions like anger, fear, and sorrow through patience, forgiveness, and hope. Emotional resilience helps individuals remain stable under pressure.

- **Key Elements**:
    - **Sabr** (Patience)
    - **Afw** (Forgiveness)
    - **Husn al-Dhann** (Hope and Optimism)
    - **Resilience in Overcoming Fear**

System Role: The Emotional Core acts as a stabilizer, ensuring individuals can control emotional responses. It supports both the spiritual and social cores, fostering peace and preventing emotional exhaustion.

4. Social Core

Definition: Social resilience draws on relationships and communal bonds to provide support during hardship. Strong family ties and community networks offer collective strength.

- **Key Elements**:
    - **Ummah** (Community Support)
    - **Silat al-Rahm** (Family Ties)
    - **Ukhuwah** (Brotherhood and Sisterhood)

System Role: The Social Core functions as the support network, providing external reinforcement for individual resilience. It works as a feedback system, where individuals draw strength from relationships and contribute back to the community.

5. Behavioral Core

Definition: This category focuses on actions and discipline aligned with Islamic principles. Obedience to Allah's commandments and maintaining balance through moderation are central to resilience.

- **Key Elements**:
    - **Ita'at Allah** (Obedience to Allah)
    - **Wasatiyyah** (Moderation and Balance)

System Role: The Behavioral Core ensures practical alignment with spiritual and cognitive principles. It drives actions that reflect resilience, keeping behavior consistent even in adversity.

6. Physical Core

Definition: Physical resilience ensures the body is maintained as a trust from Allah, enabling consistent worship, work, and social engagement. Health is treated as a foundation for enduring trials.

- **Key Elements**:
    - **Afiya** (Physical Well-Being)
    - **Rest, Nutrition, and Physical Endurance**

System Role: The Physical Core ensures the stamina required for engaging in spiritual, emotional, and social activities. It supports the long-term sustainability of other resilience dimensions.

7. Economic Core

Definition: Economic resilience focuses on managing wealth and resources wisely while trusting in Allah's provision. Charity ensures that personal wealth contributes to societal well-being.

- **Key Elements**:
    - **Zakat and Sadaqah** (Charity)
    - **Rizq** (Provision and Trust in Allah's Sustenance)

System Role: The Economic Core ensures financial stability, which reduces stress and strengthens social bonds through generosity. It helps balance worldly concerns with spiritual goals.

8. Adaptive Core

Definition: Adaptive resilience emphasizes continuous growth and flexibility in the face of changing circumstances. It involves perseverance, spiritual purification, and repentance.

- **Key Elements**:
    - **Mujahada** (Perseverance)
    - **Tazkiyah** (Purification)
    - **Tawbah** (Repentance)

System Role: The Adaptive Core ensures the system evolves, encouraging individuals to learn from mistakes and adapt to new challenges. It fosters growth through purification and repentance.

9. Integrative Core: Hope and Trust (Tawakkul and Qadr)

Definition: The integrative core ensures that all other cores align with the belief in Allah's plan (Qadr) and trust in His wisdom (Tawakkul). This core provides a sense of peace and purpose.

- **Key Elements**:
    - **Tawakkul** (Trust in Allah)
    - **Qadr** (Divine Predestination)

System Role: The Integrative Core connects all dimensions, ensuring that every action and response aligns with the belief that everything is part of Allah's greater plan. It helps individuals stay calm during uncertainty and strengthens other cores by providing meaning.

Interconnections Between Categories

- **Feedback Loops**: A key aspect of systems thinking is feedback loops. For example, spiritual resilience feeds emotional resilience. When one firmly believes in Allah's plan (Tawakkul, Qadr), they can better manage emotional stress (Sabr, Rida). Similarly, a supportive community (Ummah, Ukhuwah) reinforces emotional resilience and ethical conduct, which in turn strengthens the social fabric.

- **Emergence**: The whole is greater than the sum of its parts. These elements interact to produce emergent resilience; a holistic strength that could not be achieved by focusing on one dimension alone. For example, the simultaneous cultivation of patience (Sabr), spiritual submission (Tasleem), and social bonds (Ummah) generates greater overall resilience than these traits alone.

The Framework: A Living, Adaptive System

The **Divine Resilience Model (DRM)** works like an **ecosystem**; a set of interdependent subsystems that reinforce each other through **feedback loops**. When one core strengthens, it feeds energy back into the system, sustaining the whole. Here's how the DRM functions:

1. **Inputs**:
   The Spiritual Core provides the initial input; belief in Tawheed and sincere intention shape all actions.

2. **Processes**:
   The Cognitive, Emotional, and Behavioral Cores act as processing systems, determining how challenges are interpreted and responded to. Physical health

ensures endurance, while economic stability reduces external stress.

3. **Outputs**:
   The Social Core provides external feedback, while the Adaptive Core ensures continuous improvement. The Integrative Core aligns all actions with divine purpose.

The Divine Resilience Model

By dividing these elements into nine interconnected areas; Spiritual, Cognitive, Emotional, Social, Behavioral, Physical, Economic, Adaptive, and Integrative; we can envision a holistic resilience model rooted in the profound wisdom of the Quran. This model highlights that resilience transcends mere endurance of hardship, instead focusing on spiritual, emotional, and social flourishing within the framework of Islamic ethics and faith. Reflecting life's interconnectedness, this model harmonizes spiritual, cognitive, emotional, social, behavioral, physical, and economic dimensions. Anchored by Tawheed and maintained through balanced feedback systems, it ensures continuous growth amidst trials.

Ultimately, a Divine Resilience Theory, grounded in systems thinking, portrays resilience as a dynamic, multifaceted process, where inner strength (spiritual resilience) and outward actions (social, moral, and material resilience) reinforce each other, fostering a balanced and holistic path to thriving despite adversity.

Final Inner Dialogues

Let us counsel one another in truth, and let patience be our constant guide. When I share advice, understand it does not stem from a place of superiority, but from a heart that desires only what is best for us.

Through my exploration to Quran, I have to share these inner dialogues

Blind Hearts, Perfect Universe

It is baffling how some believe that the universe; a symphony of flawless precision; arose from random chance. This cosmic harmony, balanced on the edge of perfection, reflects a design so intricate that even the tiniest disturbance would unravel it. What we grasp through our limited understanding; whether at the grand scale of galaxies or down to the atomic level; is just the surface. Surely, the layers of precision run even deeper, far beyond our comprehension.

The moon glides through its orbit like a dancer in perfect rhythm, neither faltering nor drifting away. The Earth rests precisely where it must, nestled in the delicate balance of distance, gravity, and atmosphere. And the sun, a blazing beacon, remains stationed in its appointed place, its energy neither overwhelming nor insufficient. Were any of these elements to shift even slightly; by a margin thinner than a hair; life as we know it would collapse into chaos. Yet, this grand orchestration endures, unchanged and unblemished over millennia.

Even more astonishing is that many of those who dismiss divine design are hailed as the brightest among us; thinkers with towering IQs, celebrated for their brilliance. Still, they argue that all this arose by sheer probability, a stroke of random luck. The odds? One in trillions, perhaps more. And not just the creation of this system but its ongoing maintenance; flawless and uninterrupted across the ages. It's akin to someone claiming that the phone in your hand assembled itself, pixel by pixel, circuit by circuit, with all its apps and functionalities arising purely by accident. And even if such a miracle were possible, could this self-made phone update itself, sustain its performance, and remain functional for years to come; just as the universe seems to do without fault?

But Allah teaches us that this blindness is not of the eyes but of the heart.

> *"It is not the eyes that grow blind, but the hearts within the chests"* (Quran 22:46).

This spiritual blindness is rooted in arrogance, a stubborn refusal to acknowledge the Creator. It is not the lack of evidence that keeps them from belief, but the reluctance to accept accountability. For to admit the existence of a Creator is to accept that one's life must follow a moral order, governed by divine guidance. Yet many prefer the illusion of freedom; content to drift in what they believe to be chaos, unwilling to bow to the truth.

True wisdom lies in recognizing that the order we observe is not accidental. The precision of the universe speaks louder than any theory of randomness. Every atom, every orbit, every law of physics points to a purpose and a Planner. It is not intelligence alone that leads to truth, but humility; the willingness to open the heart to what the eyes cannot see. To deny the signs written across the universe is to blind oneself to reality.

Indeed, the universe is a mirror reflecting the greatness of its Creator, reminding us that everything, from the smallest grain to the farthest star, follows His command. The more we explore, the more we realize how perfectly everything fits, leaving no room for chaos, only awe. And the question remains: Will we recognize the signs, or will we, too, let the arrogance of our hearts shroud us from the truth?

For the wise, every sunrise, every orbit, every breath is a testament; not to randomness, but to the One who created, sustains, and commands all things in perfect harmony.

Why we were created?

Let us pause, breathe, and return to the source; our Creator. The question of why we were created has puzzled philosophers, scientists, and thinkers across centuries. But the answer lies not in speculation, but in the words of the One who fashioned us. In Surah Adh-Dhariyat (51:56), Allah declares:

"And I did not create the jinn and mankind except to worship Me."

This verse offers profound clarity: the essence of our existence is worship. Yet, worship goes beyond rituals; it encompasses living in obedience, gratitude, and awareness of Allah in every moment. Worship is not confined to prayer mats but flows into every breath, word, and action; living consciously, with purpose. While theologians embrace this divine explanation, many people seek meaning through human intellect; philosophizing life's purpose through existential, metaphysical, or psychological lenses. This habit of overestimating the self is as old as humanity itself: we tend to believe we are superior in understanding, but in reality, we are not.

Here lies a paradox. Humanity is neither the strongest nor the most obedient of creation. Angels surpass us in their unwavering submission to Allah. Animals are stronger, and the heavens more majestic. Yet, despite our weaknesses, we occupy a position that is both honored and humbling. As Allah reveals in Surah Al-Jathiyah (45:13):

> *"And He has subjected to you whatever is in the heavens and whatever is on the earth; all from Him. Indeed, in that are signs for a people who reflect."*

From the tiniest ant beneath our feet to the fiercest predator in the wild, every creature in creation has the potential to disrupt our lives. Whether it's a mosquito buzzing in the night, a snake slithering in silence, or a virus too small to see, each one carries the power to upend our world. They outnumber us, overwhelm us, and, in moments of weakness, remind us how fragile we are. Even without conscious thought or intention, these beings—some without a brain, like viruses—can bring nations to their knees, shattering our sense of control.

We like to believe that human strength, intellect, and ingenuity place us at the top of creation's hierarchy. But every time an invisible pathogen forces us into isolation or a swarm of insects devastates entire fields, we are reminded that dominance is an illusion. No amount of power, no stroke of brilliance, can guarantee us immunity from nature's unpredictable forces.

It is not our mind, strength, or effort that ultimately keeps us safe. It is the Creator—the One who fashioned everything seen and unseen, from the largest of galaxies to the tiniest of microorganisms. He is the One who grants us protection, allows us to prevail, and holds the balance between what could harm us and what could pass us by. Without His will, even the smallest creature could make life unbearable. It's not our technology or wisdom that preserves us but the mercy and mastery of the One who sustains all things.

In recognizing this truth, humility becomes our strength. We understand that being human does not place us above nature but within it, reliant on the same Creator who shaped every living thing. This recognition shifts our perspective—from pride in our achievements to gratitude for the unseen mercy that shields us from forces beyond our control. We walk not in arrogance but in awe, knowing that the One who holds all creation in His hand is the only true source of security and peace.

This is the wisdom: strength lies not in domination but in submission—submission to the Creator's will. And in that surrender, we find not weakness but resilience, for the One who created all things is also the One who sustains and protects those who place their trust in Him.

This subjugation is not an endorsement of our strength but a reminder of the trust placed upon us. Everything around us; the brilliance of the sun, the strength of beasts, the wonders of nature; exists to serve us, not for indulgence, but to support us in fulfilling the spiritual responsibility given by Allah.

The heavens, earth, and mountains declined this weighty trust, fearing its burden, as mentioned in Surah Al-Ahzab (33:72).

> *33:72 Indeed, we offered the Trust to the heavens and the earth and the mountains, and they declined to bear it and feared it; but man [undertook to] bear it. Indeed, he was unjust and ignorant.*

But we, fragile humanity, accepted it. This acceptance brings both honor and accountability, a sacred duty to live in alignment with Allah's will.

Yet, how easily we forget. Some grow arrogant, believing they are beyond consequence. In Surah Al-Qiyamah (75:36), Allah warns:

> *"Does man think that he will be left neglected?"*

This rhetorical question strikes at the heart of human arrogance. Do we believe we can live without accountability, as if our actions bear no weight in the grand design? A similar warning echo in Surah Al-Balad (90:5):

> *"Does he think that never will anyone overcome him?"*

Here lies the tragedy of arrogance; forgetting our place in the order of things. Pharaoh, in his delusion, claimed divinity, believing himself master over life and death, earth and sky. But where is he now? Reduced to a mummified corpse, displayed behind glass in a museum; a silent testimony to the foolishness of human pride. His power crumbled, his name became a lesson, not a legacy.

We, who sometimes see ourselves as invincible, are in truth fragile and fleeting. The human body, so dependent on food, water, and even basic comforts; a toilet, perhaps even toilet paper; cannot survive without Allah's provision. A mere mosquito, no bigger than a grain of rice, could topple even the mightiest of us, bringing our grandest plans to a halt. How tragic it is to think we are gods, yet so dependent on the smallest blessings.

The world, in all its beauty and complexity, has been placed under our care not to glorify us, but to guide us back to Allah. Every sunrise, every creature, every breath is a sign pointing to our Creator. This life, with its joys and hardships, is a test; a preparation for what lies beyond. As much as we are honored to carry this trust, we must remember that everything revolves around fulfilling our divine mission: to worship, obey, and recognize Allah's sovereignty in all that we do.

Know Your Place. When Allah asks, "Does man think that he will be left neglected?" we should pause and reflect deeply. Life is not a playground of indulgence, nor a stage for our egos. It is a sacred journey; every choice, every moment, weighed and accounted for. Those who ignore this truth walk a path of delusion, much like Pharaoh, whose arrogance was his undoing.

In the end, all will return to their Creator. The wise among us are those who recognize that the true measure of greatness is not found in power, wealth, or intellect, but in humility before Allah. We were created for a purpose far greater than worldly pursuits. And that purpose, woven into every fiber of our being, is to worship Him; in prayer, in action, and in every breath.

So, let us know our place, for the One who created us already told us why we exist. The world is not ours to conquer, but a reminder of the One to whom we must return. In knowing this, we find our peace, our purpose, and our place in the grand design of creation.

Fragile Minds, Divine Guidance

The human mind is both a marvel and a mystery; capable of genius but easily swayed, prone to wander even as it seeks truth. Astonishingly, nearly one-third of humanity believes a man to be God or the son of God; not because he asked for worship, but because they insist upon it. This reveals a strange paradox: our brilliance often stumbles when discerning right from wrong. Even scientists, armed with vast knowledge, sometimes hold fast to the idea that the universe came from mere randomness; a cosmic accident without intention.

Consider the story of Prophet Ibrahim (peace be upon him). Confronted with the absurdity of idol worship, he searched for the truth. He declared the moon his god; until it vanished into the night. Then he looked to the sun, larger and brighter, only to find it too would set. His brilliant mind could only take him so far, leading him in circles until he prayed for divine guidance. And only then did the Lord reveal the truth to him, showing that human intellect, no matter how sharp, is limited without a higher light to follow.

The Christmas story offers another vivid example of how the human mind twists even sacred teachings. What began as a celebration of Jesus's birth; intended to honor values like peace, love, and humility; gradually morphed over centuries. Foreign customs and pre-Christian traditions seeped in, taking the holiday far from its original purpose. It wasn't long before commercial giants saw profit in the festivities. Coca-Cola, for example, reimagined Saint Nicholas into Santa Claus in the 1930s, dressing him in the now-iconic red suit, branding the season with consumerism.

Step by step, the focus shifted. What was once a solemn reflection on faith has become a whirlwind of materialism, holiday sales, and lavish parties. Today, the Christmas season is often marked by excess: drinking, nudity, and behaviors far removed from anything Jesus would have taught or accepted. It's startling that many children born in September for single moms come from the reckless behavior of these celebrations; evidence of a holiday that has wandered far from faith. May Allah guide all to the right path. It is, perhaps, the devil's perfect plan: a slow and patient diversion that transforms something sacred into a season of indulgence, all under the guise of tradition.

But this twisting of truth is not exclusive to Christianity. In Islam, we see a similar drift with Sufism. Tasawwuf began as a pure movement focused on asceticism, self-purification, and detachment from worldly desires. Early Sufis sought divine love through simplicity and humility, striving to transcend the ego. Over time, however, some Sufi practices incorporated music, poetry, and even dance; such as the whirling of the Mevlevi dervishes; transforming what was once spiritual devotion into cultural performance. One must wonder: How would Prophet Muhammad (peace be upon him) or his companions respond if they saw such practices? Would they be pleased with rituals that drift so far from the simplicity of the original message?

These examples; and many others; reveal a sobering truth: the human mind alone cannot reliably navigate toward the divine. It twists, drifts, and gets lost in cultural norms and personal desires. We must turn back to the source if we seek the truth. And who could be more trustworthy as a guide than the Creator Himself?

The Qur'an reminds us:

> "It is not for a believing man or a believing woman, when Allah and His Messenger have decided a matter, that they should [thereafter] have any choice about their affair. And whoever disobeys Allah and His Messenger has certainly strayed into clear error."
> (Surah Al-Ahzab 33:36)

Even plants, though mindless, instinctively bend toward the light when enclosed in darkness. A small hole is all they need to find their way. If something without reason can find the light, how can we; blessed with intellect; fail to follow the truth that is so clearly within reach?

The answer lies in humility. While the mind is a powerful tool, it is not infallible. Wisdom teaches that intellect, however refined, is limited. Without divine guidance, even the sharpest mind will wander; like Ibrahim searching among the stars or humanity celebrating Santa instead of the Savior. True wisdom begins not with knowing everything, but with acknowledging the limits of our understanding and seeking the light from the One who created us.

Without that guidance, we stumble, grasping at shadows. But with it, we walk in light, aligned with the purpose for which we were made.

In the Shadow of Eternity: The Six Stages of Human Existence

There's a hidden gem in the Quran, a verse that echoes across time and invites us to ponder our origin and destiny.

Surah Al-A'raf, 7:172, unravels a profound truth:

> *"And [mention] when your Lord took from the children of Adam - from their loins - their descendants and made them testify of themselves, [saying to them], 'Am I not your Lord?' They said, 'Yes, we have testified' – lest you should say on the Day of Resurrection, 'Indeed, we were unaware of this.'"*

This verse draws me deeper, like a current beneath the surface of a vast ocean. It makes me reflect on the six stages of our existence; each one a marker in the grand story of life, from our beginning to our eternal end. These stages weave the fabric of our journey: The Atoms Stage, The Age of Exemption, The Age of Responsibility, The Stage of the Grave, The Age of Reckoning, and Eternal Life.

The First Stage: The Atoms Stage

In a realm beyond human memory, the souls of every descendant of Adam were gathered. Before we were even bodies in the world, we bore witness to the oneness of Allah, recognizing Him as the Sovereign of all things. In this moment, we existed as tiny specks, like ants among mountains, acknowledging our Creator's oneness.

But we forgot; because that is the nature of the human soul. Just as we struggle to recall the trivial details of last month's breakfast, we cannot remember that primordial moment. Yet it is imprinted in our spiritual DNA, waiting to resurface when we awaken to faith.

The Second Stage: The Age of Exemption

This is the time from conception to adulthood, a phase when accountability has yet to begin. From the safety of the womb to childhood's carefree days, we are exempt from divine responsibility. In Islam, this phase ends not at a fixed number but with physical signs: menstruation for girls, nocturnal emissions for boys, and the growth of pubic hair; ushering in adulthood. Roughly around fifteen years for most, this phase is brief, yet profound, laying the foundation for what follows.

The Third Stage: The Age of Responsibility

This stage is our test. With adulthood comes the burden of choice; between right and wrong, prayer and neglect, fasting and indulgence. This is the era in which deeds are measured, the period we spend in conscious worship or heedlessness. On average, this life may span 50 years. But if we subtract the hours spent sleeping, eating, and working, the time available for worship shrinks drastically; leaving us with merely a few productive years to secure our eternal destiny.

This fleeting stage holds immense significance. How we live it determines everything that comes after. It is the critical window to trade this temporary world for the eternal.

The Fourth Stage: The Stage of the Grave (Barzakh)

When the body returns to the earth, the soul enters Barzakh; the realm between death and resurrection. Here, time takes on a new form. For some, this phase will be peaceful; for others, it will be torment. In this interlude, we begin to grasp where we stand; whether destined for paradise or the fires of hell. Though it can last thousands of years for the earliest descendants of Adam, it is but a blink in the span of eternity.

The Fifth Stage: The Age of Reckoning

This stage begins with the blast of Israfil's trumpet, calling all souls to rise. On the Day of Judgment, every action, every whisper of intention, will be laid bare before the Almighty. There will be no intermediaries, no veils; just the naked truth beneath the gaze of the Most Just. As the Quran describes, this day will span 50,000 years:

> *"The angels and the Spirit ascend to Him in a Day the measure of which is fifty thousand years." (Surah Al-Ma'arij, 70:4)*

May Allah, in His infinite mercy, ease this day for us and grant us entry into Jannah without reckoning.

The Sixth Stage: Eternal Life

After judgment, the final stage unfolds; one of eternal reward or eternal punishment. The righteous will ascend to paradise, a realm where joy knows no bounds. There, pleasures exceed imagination; endless, uninterrupted, and beyond what the heart could ever desire. Time ceases to exist; there is no count of years, no end to the experience.

For the wicked, however, the flames of hell are an unrelenting reality. This is the final destination; forever.

When you contemplate these stages, reason leads to a single conclusion: we must live for the eternal life to come. What value does a century of worldly life hold when the first fifteen years are spent in innocence, and the last thirty often in weakness and decline? Subtract sleep, work, and distractions, and what remains for worship is but a sliver.

This world is fleeting, and its pleasures are built on deprivation. When we finally achieve what we desire, the satisfaction fades. One of the hidden blessings of prohibitions in Islam is that they keep us from becoming too attached to temporary pleasures, preserving our hearts for the greater joy that awaits in the hereafter.

We are, each of us, like merchants trading our lives. Some invest in good deeds and profit, while others squander their opportunities and lose everything. The Prophet Muhammad (PBUH) advised us wisely:

> *"Be in this world as if you were a stranger or a traveler passing through."*

A traveler may enjoy the sights and experiences of a foreign land, but he never forgets that his real home lies elsewhere. Similarly, we should engage with the world, but not cling to it. Our true destination is the hereafter, and every step we take in this life should bring us closer to paradise.

Choose Your Trade Wisely. In the shadow of eternity, the six stages of human existence illuminate the path we must follow. This life; though it feels long; is but a brief test. The choices we make during the Age of Responsibility echo through the ages, determining our fate in the eternal life that awaits.

So, reflect deeply. Will you trade this fleeting world for an everlasting paradise? Or will you cling to its fading pleasures, only to find that they slip through your grasp? In every moment, with every action, we shape our destiny. Choose wisely, for the gates of eternity swing open to those who prepare for them.

Seek enlighten

Seek enlightenment among the verses of the Quran, for within them lie the secrets of existence; an eternal rhythm of opposites that calls us to reflection and renewal. One such verse shines with unmatched clarity, whispering wisdom that echoes through time. It is a beacon for those who pause to listen, drawing the seeker deeper with each meditation.

Surah Ash-Shams (91:1-10) reveals:

"By the sun and its brightness;
And [by] the moon when it follows it;
And [by] the day when it displays it;
And [by] the night when it covers it;
And [by] the sky and He who
constructed it;
And [by] the earth and He who spread
it;
And [by] the soul and He who
proportioned it;
And inspired it [with discernment of] its
wickedness and its righteousness;
He has succeeded who purifies it;

> *And he has failed who instills it [with corruption]."*

Here, the Quran offers us a cosmic map; the interplay of light and shadow, good and evil, calling us to reflect on the nature of our own souls. The sun and moon, the day and night, the sky above and the earth below; each pair reflects a duality we embody, an inner tension that must be resolved. The unconscious and conscious mind, spirit and matter, darkness and light; they are not enemies but companions in a divine dance. The moon hides in night what the sun reveals by day, just as our waking minds carry what the soul silently knows.

So too with the self: a delicate composition shaped by God, given both the inclination toward wickedness and the capacity for righteousness. Within this inner landscape, a spark awaits; an illumination that, when nurtured, becomes the guiding light. Like the Prophet Muhammad (PBUH), who ventured into the cave's darkness and emerged with the light of monotheism, each of us must face the night within to discover the truth that God places in our hearts.

The path of Islam is that light; a path of purification, where the soul finds healing and meaning. He who purifies himself through faith, intention, and good deeds thrives, for he aligns with the natural order, reflecting the brightness of the sun in his soul. But he who allows his soul to be corrupted, who denies the light within and clings to darkness, falls into ruin.

Faith is not inherited through lineage, nor secured through status. It is a gift from God, a grace that can only enter a heart ready to receive it. And for this readiness, one must be vigilant against the four roots of wrongdoing:

- **Exaltation:** *"I am better than him,"* declared Satan, blinded by pride.

- **Arrogance:** *"Who is more powerful than us?"* challenged the people of 'Ad, only to be destroyed.

- **Tyranny:** *"I only show you what I see,"* claimed Pharaoh, intoxicated with power.

- **Vanity:** *"I was only given it because of my knowledge,"* boasted Qarun, unaware that his wealth was but a trial.

These are the shadows that obscure the light of faith; pride, arrogance, tyranny, and vanity. They corrupt the soul, closing the heart to truth. Avoid these traps, and your heart will soften, becoming fertile ground for divine light to grow.

The essence of this journey is to see yourself reflected in the cosmic order. Just as day follows night and the moon gives way to the sun, purification must follow temptation, and light must conquer darkness. With each moment of self-awareness, you draw closer to God's grace, aligning your heart with the rhythms of creation.

Success lies not in wealth, power, or status but in the quiet, persistent effort to cleanse the heart; to heal what is broken, to let light enter, and to thrive. As the Quran says, *"He has succeeded who purifies it."* This is the essence of life: a journey from darkness to light, from division to unity, from corruption to purity.

In the end, every soul will stand before its Creator, with the light it nurtured or the darkness it embraced. So, when the spark of truth touches your heart, do not turn away. The soul that seeks enlightenment, like the moon trailing the sun, will always find its way.

The Divine's Call for Humankind

Life is a journey along paths marked by choices, trials, and subtle whispers from the Divine. In this dance between free will and destiny, the call from Allah unfolds in stages; each one an invitation, urging the soul to return. This call, intertwined with patience, can be likened to waves; sometimes gentle, sometimes forceful, but always purposeful. Patience is not merely about waiting but about knowing how to act, how to endure, and how to trust. Through these stages, Allah's guidance is an invitation to align our actions, emotions, and acceptance with His will. The rhythm of divine patience is woven into four forms:

Stage 1: The Gentle Whisper; Guidance Offered

The journey begins with subtle signs; those fleeting moments of clarity: a kind word, a meaningful verse, or even an inspiring video stumbled upon by chance. These signs are soft nudges from Allah, urging us to recognize the truth and align with His guidance. Humans invent the means, but it is Allah who gives us hearts to perceive and intellect to understand. This stage invites us to avoid disobedience with ease, steering us toward good without hardship. Yet, if we ignore these whispers, the call becomes louder.

Stage 2: The Loving Discipline; Trials That Teach

When we fail to heed the gentle whisper, Allah's love shifts to discipline. As a parent corrects a beloved child, Allah brings challenges into our lives; not to harm but to nurture. Problems and setbacks arrive as opportunities to develop strength, patience, and clarity. This is the stage of patience in obedience; holding firm in worship and goodness, even when life feels heavy. Just as the companions of the Prophet endured hardship to become stronger, we too are invited to rise through the tests, growing more resilient with each trial.

Stage 3: The Wake-Up Call; A Trial Unavoidable

If the second stage is ignored, Allah's call becomes undeniable. This time, it may come as a personal crisis; sickness, loss, or emotional struggle; forcing us to confront our reality. There is no escape from these trials. They serve as wake-up calls, inviting us to reflect, repent, and realign with the Divine will. Here, patience with the decree of Allah becomes essential, as we learn to surrender and trust His wisdom in the face of difficulty. These trials are reminders, urging us to return before the greater reckoning.

Stage 4: The Final Abandonment; Freedom to Fall

The most severe fate is not loss or hardship but indifference. When all prior calls are ignored, Allah may let a person go, allowing them to chase worldly desires without restriction. This may seem like freedom, but it is a silent catastrophe. The heart becomes disconnected from its Creator, lost in distractions, and blinded by fleeting pleasures. Allah warns,

> *"Do not be like those who forgot Allah, so He made them forget themselves"*
> *(Quran 59:19).*

To forget Allah is to forget who we are, drifting away from our purpose and ending with nothing to show in the hereafter.

So, if we are wise enough; we would answer the call before time runs out. Each of these stages is an invitation to return, to embrace the rhythm of divine patience: resisting temptation, staying obedient through trials, and surrendering to Allah's decree. The choice to respond lies with us. Even in the final moments, the door to return remains open, for Allah's mercy is boundless. By practicing patience in all its forms, we align with the Divine's plan and discover the blessings of both this world and the next.

May we recognize the signs, embrace the trials, and respond to the call with open hearts; before it is too late.

Why Faith is a Gift, Not a Given?

What you see happening today; all this chaos, confusion, and noise; is nothing new. Our Creator knew it long before and sent prophets to remind us of our origins, our purpose, and our place in the universe. You might wonder, "Why did God choose just a few among us? Why not reveal Himself directly?" The answer lies deeper than mere logic; it's woven into the nature of existence itself. Let me explain it in a way we can all relate to; and to Allah belongs the highest example.

Think of how electricity reaches your home. At the source, the generator produces energy at a voltage so powerful that if it came to you directly, it would burn everything in its path. To make it useful, we rely on transformers and conductors, stepping the power down, little by little, until it reaches our homes safely. Now, consider the Divine; God's essence is far greater than we could ever comprehend, a force infinite in its purity and power. We might think ourselves clever or capable, but approaching Him without preparation would overwhelm and destroy us, much like trying to handle raw electricity with bare hands.

This is why God, in His mercy, sent messengers; prophets, much like transformers; chosen to carry that divine light and transmit it to us in ways we can bear.

Prophets receive the commands from angels, who themselves are vessels strong enough to receive and carry God's word. Through the prophets, that pure light is filtered and transformed, made accessible to human hearts. It's not because we are unworthy; it's because we are fragile. And the irony is that many of us, in our arrogance, refuse to recognize this. We think we can grasp everything on our own, forgetting the infinite distance between our understanding and His wisdom.

Take a moment to reflect on the vastness of the universe. You are but a grain of sand in an endless desert, a single speck amidst the vast Sahara. Yet we let pride swell in our hearts, making it hard to accept that there is a Creator far beyond us, one who understands all that we do not. This pride becomes a barrier, a wall between us and faith, making it easy to question, doubt, and resist the message when it arrives.

Allah has sent prophets to free those whom He wills from the worship of creation to the worship of the Creator, from the narrowness of this world to its vastness, and from the injustice of false religions to the justice of Islam.

And here is where many misunderstand the nature of faith: it isn't something inherited, nor is it guaranteed by proximity to holiness. Even the most righteous surroundings cannot force belief into an unwilling heart. Look at the story of Prophet Noah. For nearly a thousand years, he called his people to the truth, yet his own son turned away, blinded by arrogance. In the end, Noah's son drowned not just in water but in disbelief, his heart too heavy with pride to rise to faith.

Then there's the story of Prophet Lut's wife. She lived beside a prophet, shared his household, and witnessed his message firsthand; yet she betrayed him, her heart tethered to disbelief. Proximity to holiness didn't save her because faith isn't inherited by mere association; it must be awakened within.

And what of Abu Talib, the uncle of Prophet Muhammad? He stood by his nephew, protected him, and admired him, but in his final moments, he chose to remain with the ways of his forefathers. Even with the Prophet at his side, urging him to declare faith, the pride of tradition and the presence of men like Abu Jahl held him back. His heart clung to what was familiar, unable to release itself into the unknown beauty of belief.

Faith, therefore, is not a birthright. It is a gift; a delicate flame that must be nurtured with humility, sincerity, and openness. It doesn't matter how close you stand to the light if you refuse to open your eyes to see it. Even if your father were a prophet or your household steeped in righteousness, that alone would not guarantee your faith. The heart must bow before the mind can believe.

In this lies the profound truth: faith is not something we control or command. It comes to those who seek it with humility, who understand that the mind alone cannot fathom the fullness of the Divine. To receive faith is to admit that we do not have all the answers, to embrace the mystery of life and trust in the One who does. And that is why faith is not a given; it is a gift. It requires a heart that is willing to let go of pride, surrender to something greater, and walk with trust even when the path is unclear.

We may strive, we may resist, but in the end, faith comes to those who realize their need for it. Like rain that falls on both barren and fertile ground, it touches everyone. But only the soil that softens to receive it will see flowers bloom. And so, the question we must each ask is: will I open my heart to the rain? Will I let go of my arrogance and allow faith to grow within me?

The gift of faith is offered to all; but only those with open hands and humble hearts will receive it.

The Gentle Balance

This faith flows gently, like a river designed to nourish the soul. Islam is inherently easy, a path made for balance, not burden. The Prophet Muhammad (PBUH) warned that if anyone tries to force the river to rush; by overburdening themselves with extremes; eventually, it will overwhelm them. To walk this path of wisdom is to follow the middle way, one of calm persistence and moderation. Seek true knowledge from the Quran and authentic Hadith. Without the right knowledge, one risks drifting away from the current of guidance, lost in the rapids of excess or neglect.

The essence of the journey is to come close to Allah, tread straight on His path, and share the beauty of faith with others. Sustaining this journey, however, requires more than good intentions; it demands prayer at dawn, in the fading light of afternoon, and in the quiet moments of the night. These acts of devotion anchor the soul, providing strength against life's inevitable tides.

As Abu Hurairah (RA) reported, the Prophet (PBUH) said: "The religion is easy, and whoever makes the religion a burden, it will overpower him. So, follow a middle course, or come close to it, and give glad tidings. Seek help at morn, at dusk, and in some part of the night" (Riyad as-Salihin 145).

This wisdom is a remedy for extremism of any kind, a reminder that causing harm to others cannot become normalized. It is sad but true; I see now death is easy but love is hard. In an era where people act on impulse and self-interest, those who hold onto their faith with sincerity are the truly wise. The wise one is not the one who succumbs to anger or fleeting desires but the one who aims for eternal life.

True guidance lies in the middle ground; holding firmly to the Qur'an and authentic Hadith without falling into neglect or exaggeration. The Qur'an is a book without doubt, a guide to the most upright way of living. It illuminates the path forward with clarity, while the Sunnah serves as its explanation, as Allah says:

> *"To make clear to the people what was sent down to them."*

Whoever clings to both the Qur'an and Sunnah, unwavering and uncorrupted, will eventually find certainty and peace.

Yet, the journey to such clarity takes time. Every soul will face struggles: inner desires that tempt, thoughts that distract, and external forces that mislead. These challenges are the furnace in which patience is forged. Steadfastness grows not in a day but in gradual steps; by holding onto the teachings, despite the pressures of the world, one becomes grounded in faith, certainty, and peace.

Consider the wisdom in the Prophet's (PBUH) handling of the Treaty of Hudaybiyyah. Though no swords clashed and no treasures were gained, it was one of the most blessed moments in Islamic history. Through restraint, patience, and trust in Allah's will, the treaty paved the way for the peaceful conquest of Mecca. No force was needed; just as Hudaybiyyah had shown, true victories come not from material conquest but from submission, peace, and mercy. This is the essence of faith: success is not measured by worldly triumphs but by the serenity found in trusting Allah's plan.

In this, there is a profound lesson: balance your efforts between the physical and the spiritual, between striving and surrender. Walk steadily, but without rushing, and seek help through prayer and patience. Hold onto love, not hatred; practice moderation, not extremes; and in all things, seek Allah's pleasure.

Trust in The Divine

Just believe in the Divine. All matters are woven by His hand, and the heart finds peace in surrender to the One who holds the threads of existence. Who else can manage the world with such wisdom, delicate yet precise? Learn from the past, for the stories in the Quran are more than just history; they are living lessons.

Consider the aching heart of Moses's mother when she placed her child into the river. Her soul felt hollow, trembling at the edge of despair. Yet Allah fortified her heart with trust, a sacred connection that carried her through. O Allah, grant us that same sacred bond; strengthen us when our own hearts waver and doubts begin to creep in. When the world grows silent and answers seem distant, help us, as You helped her, to wait patiently for what You have decreed, for in patience, we find true strength.

Through Moses, You taught us to seek not just survival but righteous endings: "Cause me to die as a Muslim, and join me with the righteous." O Allah, make us not only obedient but graceful in our submission. Be our light; not against us but for us. Let us neither harm nor be harmed, neither wound nor be wounded. Let us carry dignity through life's trials, gentle in spirit, that no one may suffer from our actions, and may we not be weighed down by the sorrows of others.

Moses, when burdened with fear, was reassured by his father-in-law's words: "Do not fear." Therein lies a precious truth; the finest gift you can offer a troubled heart is peace. It is like the ship in Surah Al-Kahf; if not damaged, it would have fallen prey to plunderers. Sometimes, what seems like harm is hidden mercy, a shield from greater loss.

Remember, Allah tests us not to break us but to refine us. Like the boy whose soul was taken to spare his parents future grief, some of His decrees are beyond our comprehension. In His withholding, there is giving; in His taking, there is protection. And the wall built to protect the orphans' treasure teaches us that divine wisdom often operates behind the veil of the unseen. With every test, every joy, and every sorrow, we whisper: O Allah, grant us patience. Teach us to trust in what we do not yet understand, for in trust lies the path to tranquility.

When hardships descend upon you, recall how Noah sailed over waves that rose like mountains, how Abraham emerged unscathed from fire's embrace. Reflect on Jonah's release from the belly of the whale and how Moses split the sea with nothing but a staff. The beauty of divine relief lies in its timing; it arrives just when all worldly hope has faded, leaving only the light of faith in the heart.

With a single prayer, Allah drowned a world in wickedness, granting victory to Noah. With a plea, He breathed life into Zechariah's barren hopes. In the dark depths of the whale's belly, He transformed it into a sanctuary for Jonah. And with a simple supplication, He turned Mecca into the spiritual compass for generations. Trust that a prayer, no matter how small, rearranges the universe in ways unseen.

It gathers what is scattered, aligns what is misaligned, and brings to life what was thought lost.

O Allah, grant us the patience of Hagar, who stood firm in a barren desert at Your command. Left alone with no water, no shelter, and no company, she asked Abraham but one thing: "Did Allah command this?" And when he said yes, she replied, "Then go, for Allah will not abandon us." O Allah, bless us with hearts as steadfast as hers, with faith as pure and unwavering. May we endure our trials with the same quiet certainty, knowing that You are enough.

Do not give up on prayers, even when the answers seem delayed. Often, Allah withholds the response to strip away our pride and purify our intentions. In that waiting, arrogance fades, and compassion grows; until we no longer look down on the disobedient with judgment but with mercy. Only when the heart is cleansed does the answer come, bringing relief untainted by self-righteousness.

We end in praise, knowing that no words can truly encompass His grace. We seek refuge in Him from doing what we once forbade others, from vanity that taints our worship, and from despising sinners when we should feel compassion. We ask protection from blessings that stir envy in our hearts and trials that shake our trust in His wisdom. In every fear and every hope, we flee from Him to Him, for there is no refuge but in His embrace.

Praise be to Allah, who calls us near with hearts trembling and eyes sincere. To Him, we bow in humble grace, prostrate before His timeless presence. No doors stand between us, no veils block our cries. The earth spreads beneath our feet, and the heavens above serve as a canopy of mercy. No mountain can rise high enough to keep His light from reaching us. The seas, though vast and deep, could never contain the ink to describe His boundless love.

Glory be to Him, the King in whose hand lies every soul and every destiny. To Him, we surrender, for He alone holds the keys to peace. His mercy encompasses all, and His wisdom directs every step. And upon His beloved Messenger, Muhammad, peace and blessings flow; he who stood through the night in prayer while others slept, tears falling as he called upon his Lord. O Allah, grant us the honor of joining him, where souls are united in eternal joy.

In paradise, where love is pure and true, we yearn to meet the beloved Prophet. O how we long to stand with him, to be among those who prostrate before their Lord in the gardens of bliss. May our journey through life be a reflection of that longing, a path paved with trust, patience, and unwavering faith in the Divine.

The Book Cover

The cover meant to embody a profound metaphor, capturing the essence of divine guidance and spiritual resilience. The radiating light symbolizes Allah's wisdom descending from the heavens, illuminating the believer's path through life's complexities. Light in the Quran represents divine knowledge and enlightenment, offering clarity and hope even in times of darkness. The open Quran at the bottom of the cover conveys accessibility and personal engagement. The interplay between the book and the heavenly light meant to simplify a continuous flow; divine wisdom informs human action, and sincere worship elevates the soul toward Allah.

The soft gold, white, and blue tones evoke purity, tranquility, and sacredness, setting the tone for peaceful contemplation. Gold hints at the timeless nature of the Quran's teachings, while blue promotes introspection. The movement within the design symbolizes that the Quran's wisdom is not static but eternal and ever-relevant to all generations. The bold typography of the title reflects clarity and accessibility, reinforcing that the Quran offers messages for everyone, regardless of background or circumstance. the signature, placed humbly at the bottom, reflects the role of the author as a conduit of these divine insights rather than the central figure, emphasizing that the wisdom within the Quran belongs to Allah alone.

Acknowledgments

In the name of Allah, the Most Compassionate, the Most Merciful, I bow my heart in gratitude to the One who shaped the heavens and the earth with precision, who grants life to every breath and meaning to every soul. To Allah belongs all praise, for without His mercy, this endeavor would be lost in the wind, scattered without purpose. Every spark of insight, every word formed, and every thought aligned is but a reflection of His boundless wisdom. It is He who guides the pen and grants clarity to the mind, for nothing moves, not even the heart, without His decree.

I extend endless gratitude to the beloved Messenger, Muhammad (PBUH), the mercy to all of creation, whose light remains a guide for every step I take. From his example flows the river of resilience and grace, teaching patience when the road is rough, humility when success tempts pride, and steadfastness when the night feels long. His life is a testament that surrender to Allah is the greatest form of freedom, and his character is a beacon reminding us that justice is not just given but lived.

Without the mercy of Allah and the example of His noble Prophet, this journey would be without meaning and this effort without substance. May every word in this work serve as a humble offering of gratitude, a small reflection of the mercy bestowed upon me. And may Allah continue to bless and guide us all along the straight path, just as He blessed His chosen ones before us.

I also acknowledge the role of technology, particularly AI tools, which supported various stages of this project.

References

Al-Bukhari, M. I. (n.d.). *Sahih al-Bukhari* (M. Muhsin Khan, Trans.). Dar-us-Salam Publications. (Original work compiled ca. 846 CE).

Ezz, Ashi. (2024). *The Bridge from Cringe to Prestige*. [Online version available at: https://a.co/d/33LZ2pm]. ISBN: 978-1-0670358-0-8.

Ezz, Ashi. (2024). *Muhammad: Lasting Resilience Model*. [Available on Amazon: https://a.co/d/e7hR0rB]. ISBN: 978-1-0670358-3-9.

The Quran. (n.d.). The Noble Quran in the English Language (Taqi-ud-Din al-Hilali & Muhammad Muhsin Khan, Trans.). King Fahd Complex for the Printing of the Holy Quran. (Original work published ca. 610–632 CE).

Sharkawi, A. (2021). *Messages from the Quran*. Kalemat

About the Author

Dr. Ashi Ezz is an expert in organizational transformation, with a doctorate specializing in risk management. Passionate about inspiring positive change, Dr. Ashi is dedicated to mentoring and coaching individuals and organizations towards better, more balanced lives. With a wealth of knowledge gained from years of practical experience, engaging with experts, and an insatiable appetite for continuous learning, Dr. Ashi is committed to empowering others to shape successful enterprises and fulfilling personal lives.

www.ingramcontent.com/pod-product-compliance
Lightning Source LLC
Chambersburg PA
CBHW030335010526
44119CB00047B/507